WAKE UP TO GOD'S WORD

WAKE UP TO GOD'S WORD

exercises for spiritual transformation

MARY H. REAMAN

ST. ANTHONY MESSENGER PRESS
Cincinnati, Ohio

Scripture passages have been taken from *New Revised Standard Version Bible*, copyright ©1989 by the Division of Christian Education of the National Council of the Churches of Christ in the U.S.A., and used by permission. All rights reserved.

Cover and book design by Mark Sullivan
Cover image ©www.istockphoto.com / Joshua Blake

LIBRARY OF CONGRESS CATALOGING-IN-PUBLICATION DATA

Reaman, Mary.
Wake up to God's word : exercises for spiritual transformation / Mary Reaman.
p. cm.
ISBN 978-0-86716-783-2 (pbk. : alk. paper) 1. Devotional literature. I. Title.

BV4832.3.R43 2007
248.4'82—dc22

2007016868

ISBN 978-0-86716-783-2

Published by St. Anthony Messenger Press
28 W. Liberty St.
Cincinnati, OH 45202
www.AmericanCatholic.org

Printed in the United States of America.
Printed on acid-free paper.

07 08 09 10 11   5 4 3 2 1

CONTENTS

To my mom and dad

It was the first day of school. Everything smelled clean and the tile floors gleamed with welcome. I was entering second grade and my teacher, Sister Marie Helen, a young Sister of Charity at the time, had crisp bright colors decorating her bulletin boards. I can still see it in my mind today as if it were yesterday. As I took my seat, my eyes rested on the long bulletin board spanning the length of the front chalkboard. Orange corrugated cardboard topped with bright yellow letters surprised me with the message: "Prayer is a friendly talk with God." I must have read that same sentence a hundred times a day that year.

That simple message opened my heart and mind to see and understand God as Friend. As a result, I began an inner dialogue with Jesus that continues to this day. I realized that if prayer was a friendly talk with God and God was my friend, then I could tell God anything and everything. I realized too, that if we were friends, then I had to be available for God. I wanted Jesus to know that I could be relied on as his friend too.

This would be one of many ways the Sisters of Charity would ignite my spiritual growth and fuel my passion for God.

Later, in the sixth grade, I was in the church practicing the art of lectoring with Sister Catherine Noreen. I remember standing at the raised lectern practicing the New Testament reading for the all-school Mass at the end of the week. As I read the Scripture, I caught Sister mouthing the words silently along with me, though she did not have the text in front of her. When I realized that she actually knew the Scripture by heart, I thought to myself, "I hope I know the Word of God by heart some day."

As I grew into adulthood and pursued my passion for theological studies earning both a master's degree and a doctorate of ministry, much of my prayer life was and continues to be guided by a phrase that resounds in the depths of my being: "Know My Word." At first, I interpreted the phrase to be a calling from God to delve more deeply into the Christian Scriptures, so I did. I became very familiar with the Gospels and continue to be lured into contemplation by their stories.

Over time as I have allowed those words to reverberate in my heart, mind and spirit, they have called me to explore more deeply my relationship with Jesus, the *Logos*, the Word of God. Following this phrase into silence, I learned how to commune with God and remain in the presence of Jesus not only while engaging in formal prayer, but also in relaxed, restful and sometimes playful ways while going about the business of my ordinary day.

Investigating the meaning of these three words while allowing them to guide my spiritual path has yielded a relationship with

God embedded in trust and bound by an intimacy that eludes description. Feeling that Jesus himself was inviting me to know him, I made it a regular practice to seek him out and talk with him, friend to friend. As I grew into this practice, I learned that listening attentively for God was a form of prayer too.

God's invitation to "Know My Word" and my response to that invitation have nurtured a life of prayer and relationship with God that continues to press my growth, demand my attention and direct my life. This book grows out of that relationship. Now I invite you to delve more deeply into your relationship with God by exploring how you can allow the Word within to guide your life, reveal your deeper potential and usher in an evolution of consciousness that honors the unity of all creation.

CHAPTER ONE

OUR JOURNEY TO FREEDOM

But Moses said to God, "If I come to the Israelites and say to them, 'The God of your ancestors has sent me to you,' and they ask me, 'What is his name?' what shall I say to them?" God said to Moses, "I AM WHO I AM." He said further, "Thus you shall say to the Israelites, 'I AM has sent me to you.' " God also said to Moses, "Thus you shall say to the Israelites, 'The LORD, the God of your ancestors, the God of Abraham, the God of Isaac, and the God of Jacob, has sent me to you':

> This is my name forever,
> and this my title for all generations.

Go and assemble the elders of Israel, and say to them, 'The LORD, the God of your ancestors, the God of Abraham, of Isaac, and of Jacob, has appeared to me, saying: I have given heed to you and to what has been done to you in Egypt. I declare that I will bring you up out of the misery of Egypt, to the land of the Canaanites, the Hittites, the Amorites, the Perizzites, the Hivites, and the Jebusites, a land flowing with milk and honey.'" (Exodus 3:13–17)

We, like the Israelites in ancient times, who left Egypt and entered into the desert to pursue freedom, are also on a journey in pursuit of freedom. Although most of us would never consider ourselves enslaved or imprisoned, we are. Enduring discontentment, conflict and violence in our personal lives and in the larger world are evidence of our enslavement. The journey of the Israelites from slavery in Egypt, through the desert and into the Promised Land characterizes our journey as well. For us, as it was for them, the journey itself is transforming, promising liberation from bondage and engendering new life altogether.

The Israelites were enslaved to Pharaoh and the Egyptians when Moses came along offering them a chance at freedom. Though the idea of freedom must have sounded promising to the Israelites, they had to know it would cost something of them to gain it. With news of Moses' willingness to lead them out of slavery, the Israelites had to discern for themselves how much they really wanted to be free. Were they willing to pay the price freedom required? Were they willing to leave the comfort of the known for the wilderness of the unknown?

Freedom may seem like an obvious and easy choice, but at least while they were in Egypt, the Israelites had permanent housing, reliable food sources and a family life and routine to which they had grown accustomed, even within the confines of slavery. If they were to follow Moses into the desert, they might be free, but they could just as easily die out there without permanent shelter and a reliable supply of food and water. Add to the equation the stress that comes with uprooting not just one household, but an entire people, as well as the tension that accompanies any transition, and the pursuit of freedom does not seem so appealing.

The decision to pursue freedom initiated immediate and rigorous change for the whole community of Israel. Their lives were deeply influenced and transformed by the experiences they had, the challenges they faced and the relationships they developed on the journey. The forty years that the Israelites traveled through the desert brought forth a multitude of heroes and heroines, as well as adversaries and opponents.

The journey of the Israelites out of Egypt into the desert and finally into the Promised Land is a metaphor for the journey of our lives. Our life journey is also a story of transformation that has the potential to bring us to a newfound freedom. Like the Israelites, we too must decide if we are willing to do whatever it takes to pursue freedom by consciously embarking on the journey of transformation.

For the Israelites, as for each of us, the journey of transformation that is the journey of our lives tests us to the point of growth. Traversing the many births, deaths and resurrections that the journey from slavery to freedom entails brings to light qualities, talents and skills in each of us that might otherwise have remained dormant. The potential contained in such hard-won discoveries may remain concealed or untapped if we continue to choose slavery by avoiding or resisting life's harsh need to change us.

Like his Jewish ancestors, Jesus embarked on a liberation journey and called others to follow him on the path to freedom. But Jesus' listeners were in denial of their enslavement. They could not fathom what Jesus was talking about when he referred to the possibility that they could be free. John's Gospel says,

> Then Jesus said to the Jews who had believed in him, "If you continue in my word, you are truly my disciples; and you will know the truth, and the truth will make you free." They answered him, "We are descendants of Abraham and have never been slaves to anyone. What do you mean by saying, 'You will be made free'?"
>
> Jesus answered them, "Very truly, I tell you, everyone who commits sin is a slave to sin. The slave does not have a permanent place in the household; the son has a place there for ever."
> (John 8:31–35)

Like others who heard Jesus' call to liberation, we have a difficult time understanding that we are not yet free. A story from the Cherokee tradition can help us gain a better understanding of this. This traditional wisdom tale, called "Two Wolves," also exposes how we participate in our own enslavement:

> A grandfather from the Cherokee nation was talking with his grandson.
>
> "A fight is going on inside me," he said to the boy. "It is a terrible fight and it is between two wolves. One wolf is evil and ugly: He is anger, envy, war, greed, self-pity, sorrow, regret, guilt, resentment, inferiority, lies, false pride, superiority, selfishness and arrogance. The other wolf is beautiful and good: He is friendly, joyful, peace, love, hope, serenity, humility, kindness, benevolence, justice, fairness, empathy, generosity, truth, compassion, gratitude and deep vision. This same fight is going on

inside you and inside every other human as well."

The grandson paused in deep reflection because of what his grandfather had just said. Then he finally cried out with concern; "Grandfather, which wolf will win?"

The elder replied, "The wolf that you feed."

The wrestling match between good and evil provides the creative tension of opposites—between yin and yang, flow and constriction, masculine and feminine—necessary for the emergence and evolution of life. These mythological wrestling matches point to an epic drama that is happening in each of us. In this book it will be referred to as a struggle between Christ consciousness and ego.

As Saint Paul said, we have "the mind of Christ" (1 Corinthians 2:16). Christ consciousness means putting on the mind of Christ. Lovingly living, not for our own sake, but for the sake of the whole of humanity is the ultimate expression of the Christ consciousness. Letting our lives be God's instrument through which healing, acceptance, reconciliation and forgiveness flow is how we put on the mind of Christ and make our way to freedom. Jesus' life and relationships mirror our lives and relationships; we can garner a great deal of insight by looking more deeply into the Scriptures and pondering Jesus' call to be free and what it means for us today.

Mary, Jesus' mother, gives us an example of what it means to bring forth Christ consciousness. She challenges us to echo her "yes" to God and to give ourselves to God to be used to bring forth the divine. In offering her life for the Incarnation, she shows us what it means to live for the sake of the whole.

By acknowledging that we have within us the capacity for both good and evil, selflessness and selfishness, generosity and stinginess, the capacity to generate and degenerate, to build up or tear down, to be merciful or judgmental, we recognize that we have both the nature of the good wolf and the evil wolf. Like Mary and Jesus, we can choose to live for the good of humanity and God by offering our lives as an unobstructed vessel for the Divine, laying bare the Christ consciousness. Or we can choose to be motivated purely by our ego, confining our lives and living for our own gratification. We have within our power the potential to manifest the Christ consciousness as well as the capacity to be self-consumed or driven by ego.

The apex of the spiritual journey is developing the ability to be free from the selfish desires that arise from our ego so that the Christ consciousness can rise up in us, come to the fore, direct our lives, transform our relationships and ignite our greatest potential. In this way we live our vocation, becoming the person God desires us to be so the world can benefit from our lives. However, before we can begin to loosen the ego's grip on us, we have to first acknowledge its presence and become familiar with the signs in our lives that reveal it is alive and well. Acknowledging the drive of the ego in our own selfish inclinations is the first step to freedom and the beginning of our transformation.

As the Cherokee tale indicates, the evil wolf expresses itself in reactive and impulsive behaviors such as greed, self-indulgence, self-pity, anger, envy, false pride and the like. It is characterized by a desire to receive for the self alone, rather than desiring to receive for the sake of sharing and the benefit of all. The negative influence of the ego manifests in both individuals and humanity as a whole, as the drive to control, manipulate, exercise power over others and exploit creation for our own gain and pleasure without any consideration for how our actions may impact and even be detrimental to the whole.

Conditioned emotional responses born of ego, such as insecurity, impatience, complacency and self-pity, influence our decisions and affect our behavior. As a result we find ourselves locked into one way of being. Unconscious emotional and behavioral patterns often keep us tied to seeing ourselves as victims and inhibit us from evolving into our potential and sharing the God-given talents and gifts with which we have been endowed for the benefit of the world.

Author Eckhart Tolle, in his recent work *A New Earth,* says the ego is the "blueprint for dysfunction that every human being carries within." According to Tolle, this dysfunction is at the root of paralyzing fear, greed and our desire for power. Unchecked, the drive of ego leads to violence and war between nations and tribes, and contributes to conflict and competition in our personal relationships.[1]

In the story of the Israelites' quest for the Promised Land, the ego is represented by Pharaoh and all things associated with their enslavement in Egypt. Throughout history, theologians, philosophers, mystics and poets have called what Tolle calls "dysfunction" and what we are calling "ego" by other names. It has also been called Satan, Lucifer, Beelzebub and Baal. Contemporary students of Jewish mysticism call the ego "the opponent."[2]

As our opponent, our ego is always ready to distract or sabotage us from pursuing our potential and actualizing the Christ consciousness. Becoming aware of the ego's drive and influence allows us to begin to contain and suppress our selfish desires, preventing the ego from being the primary determinant of our thoughts, choices and behaviors. This plays an important role in our spiritual development. By becoming adept at containing the insatiable appetite of the ego we are more able to put our energy into cultivating the nature of the good wolf while pursuing our potential, where our humanity and divinity meet and the Christ consciousness is birthed through us into the world.

The Christ consciousness is summed up in the virtues of the "good wolf" in the Cherokee tale. Like ego that exists in each one of us, the Christ consciousness also exists within each of us and expresses itself as love, generosity, compassion and forgiveness. The impulse we each have to change, grow and evolve to our highest potential is the Christ consciousness expressing itself through us and urging us to become more than we know ourselves to be. The highest expression of the Christ consciousness is a desire to receive for the sake of sharing, for the benefit of all rather than for ourselves alone. From the perspective of the Christ consciousness there is no difference between you and me, male and female, Jew, Muslim or Christian. We are all children of God.

It is important to point out that though we experience two natures there is always only *one* individual in which these two natures exist. One self hears both the call to transformation and the call to complacency. One self responds to the urging of the Christ consciousness or the urging of the ego. The choices we make determine which nature we are manifesting—which wolf we are feeding—at any given moment.

As the Cherokee tale indicates, we feed the good wolf or the bad wolf, the Christ consciousness or ego with every choice we make. Whether it is a subconscious or conscious choice, we either make that choice from the position of ego or the position of Christ consciousness. It is not possible to make a choice with one foot in ego and the other in Christ consciousness. Either we are motivated by selfishness or we are motivated by selflessness. It cannot be both. If we are motivated at all by selfishness, even if it is only a miniscule amount of selfishness, our attempt at selflessness is contaminated and we stand in union with ego. When our choices are motivated completely by selflessness, we are in union with the Christ consciousness and in communion with one another.

Unleashing the Christ consciousness is a challenging task. It is not something we do just once. It is something we have to do fifty or a hundred times a day. It is a choice of which we must be conscious every time or we are not truly choosing it and, therefore, not truly free.

Consciously choosing to embark on this journey of transformation is not for the faint of heart. If we want the world to change, if we want to be relieved of self-hatred and hatred of others, if we want an end to injustice, if we want peace in our world, workplaces, neighborhoods, homes and within, we have to set out on this path with deep passion and unshakeable desire. Only when a critical mass has attained freedom from the grip of ego will the Christ consciousness be realized in the world and the kingdom Jesus spoke about be at hand.

Pursuing a greater understanding of the Christ consciousness begins with acknowledging what Thomas Merton called "the Ground of Being," the foundation of all creation, the universal life force that birthed the cosmos, sustains every molecule, atom and cell and contains all possibilities for life's unfolding. This fundamental foundation from which all creation springs is the Word of God.

REALIZING THE WORD WITHIN

In the beginning was the Word, and the Word was with God, and the Word was God. He was in the beginning with God. All things came into being through him, and without him not one thing came into being. What has come into being in him was life, and the life was the light of all people. The light shines in the darkness, and the darkness did not overcome it.

There was a man sent from God, whose name was John. He came as a witness to testify to the light, so that all might believe through him. He himself was not the light, but he came to testify to the light. The true light, which enlightens everyone, was coming into the world.

He was in the world, and the world came into being through him; yet the world did not know him. He came to what was his own and his own people did not accept him. But to all who received him, who believed in his name, he gave power to become children of God, who were born, not of blood or of the will of the flesh or of the will of man, but of God.

And the Word became flesh and lived among us, and we have seen his glory, the glory as of a father's only son, full of grace and truth. (John 1:1-14)

The writer of John's Gospel equates the Word that has always existed and was with God from the beginning, with Jesus Christ, the "true light which enlightens everyone" (John 1:9). The writer suggests that all of creation came through the Word and contains the Word.

The text says, "...all those who received [the Word]...he gave power to become children of God..." Said another way, the Word, if we accept it, trust it and rely on it to guide our lives, empowers us to become "children of God." To be empowered is not only to recognize that we have a choice, but it also implies that we have the necessary strength and information to make a choice, though previously we might have felt there was no choice available.

If we choose to receive, accept and cultivate our awareness of the Word within ourselves and all creation, we will become like Jesus, a child of God. Conversely, we can refuse to acknowledge, deny or reject the presence of the Word within, potentially denying our relationship to it or downplaying our own divine likeness, thus becoming stagnant in our own spiritual development and missing entirely the point of life itself.

This passage from John's Gospel also points to the wrestling match that is taking place inside each one of us and between most of us. If we accept the Word, if we receive the Word within, and acknowledge its presence in ourselves and creation, the text indicates we will be enlightened. In other words, when we acknowledge and honor the Word within ourselves and all creation, we begin to see and acknowledge the unity of all things. We begin to see that the underlying reality binding everything together is the Word of God.

God's Word is contained in all creation—seen and unseen. Every relationship, circumstance and interaction in which we participate presents an opportunity to more clearly reveal or more deeply conceal the Word within it. God's Word is contained in everything. You and I, our relationships, a flower, a honeybee, our neighbor and even our enemy have the Word within. As the writer of John's Gospel claims, "...without [the Word] not one thing came into being." God's Word is not something we have to acquire. We don't have to earn it. We come with it already installed. It is fundamental to creation itself.

The Hebrew Scriptures also affirm, as John's Gospel does, that God's Word is the foundation of all life. The first chapter of Genesis states plainly that creation came forth as God's Word. The text begins with God creating the universe through ten utterances or commands. Each introductory phrase includes the words "God said" indicating that creation not only *contains* God's Word, but also that creation itself comes forth as God's Word. The text states,

> Then God said, "Let there be light"; and there was light.
>
> ...
>
> And God said, "Let there be a dome in the midst of the waters, and let it separate the waters from the waters."
>
> ...
>
> And God said, "Let the waters under the sky be gathered together into one place, and let the dry land appear."
>
> ...
>
> Then God said, "Let the earth put forth vegetation: plants yielding seed, and fruit trees of every kind on earth that bear fruit with the seed in it."

...

And God said, "Let there be lights in the dome of the sky to separate the day from the night...."

...

And God said, "Let the waters bring forth swarms of living creatures, and let birds fly above the earth across the dome of the sky."

...

And God said, "Let the earth bring forth living creatures of every kind: cattle and creeping things and wild animals of the earth of every kind."

...

Then God said, "Let us make humankind in our image, according to our likeness...."

...

God said to them, "Be fruitful and multiply, and fill the earth..."

...

God said, "See, I have given you every plant yielding seed that is upon the face of all the earth, and every tree with seed in its fruit; you shall have them for food." (Genesis 1:3, 6, 9, 11, 14, 20, 24, 26, 28, 29)

The psalmist proclaims, "By the word of the LORD the heavens were made, / and all their host by the breath of [God's] mouth" (33:6). The book of Sirach states, "By the word of the Lord [God's] works are made" (42:15). Moses, too, affirmed this in his parting speech to the Israelites, reminding them that the Word of God was not out of reach for them. He said,

Surely, this commandment that I am commanding you today is not too hard for you, nor is it too far away. It is not in heaven, that you should say, "Who will go up to heaven for us, and get it for us so that we may hear it and observe it?" Neither is it beyond the sea, that you should say, "Who will cross to the other side of the sea for us, and get it for us so that we may hear it and observe it?" No, the word is very near to you; it is in your mouth and in your heart for you to observe. (Deuteronomy 30:11–14)

When Moses reminded the Israelites that the Word of God was within them—in their mouths and in their hearts, they had only "to observe it"—he was conveying to them that the Word within, if they adhered to it and allowed it to direct their lives, could lead them to freedom and usher them into the Promised Land. Moses was right when he said to the Israelites, "The Word of God is not too remote for you." The Word is within! It is contained in us and all creation! As partners in our relationship with God, we have a responsibility to develop tools that can increase our awareness of and access to the Word that has been written in our hearts so we and the world we live in can be shaped, transformed and unbound by it.

The prophet Isaiah confirmed this when he declared:

> For as the rain and the snow come down from heaven,
>> and do not return there until they have watered the earth,
> making it bring forth and sprout,
>> giving seed to the sower and bread to the eater,
> so shall my word be that goes out from my mouth;
>> it shall not return to me empty,

>but it shall accomplish that which I purpose,
>
>and succeed in the thing for which I sent it. (Isaiah 55:10–11)

The Word within, when outwardly expressed, is the manifestation of the Christ consciousness in the world. The Christ consciousness emerges and comes through us when the intention behind our thoughts, words and deeds is rooted in and aligned with the Word within, the fundamental goodness inherent in both Creator and created. The task of our lives is not only to acknowledge and honor the Word within, but to manifest it, express it and live it out as the Christ consciousness in the world. When we are able to achieve this, the Word will have completed its task.

Remember, the writer of John's Gospel reminds us that for those who "accept the Word" and "believe in it, [God] gives them power to become children of God." We live into our identity as children of God by seeing ourselves, one another and all creation as vessels containing the Word of God. When we begin relating to one another and all creation as God's Word or an expression of God, we begin to see through the illusion of separateness to the unity of all things.

As Moses reminded the Israelites, if we allow it, the Word within will direct our lives. By developing the capacity to discern the presence of the Word within and then attempting to align our thoughts, words and deeds with it, we engage the process of becoming, thus exercising our power to become children of God. As a result we become what we were always meant to be—God's kin, God's flesh and blood, God's children.

In fact, Eckhart Tolle echoes this sentiment when he says, "You do not become good by trying to be good, but by finding the goodness that is already within you, and allowing that goodness to emerge."[3] The Word within is the goodness that is already in us. It is our essence and the ground of our being. But, Tolle warns, "[that goodness] can only emerge if something fundamental changes in your state of consciousness."[4] Changing our state of consciousness happens by taking responsibility for the choices we make. The Cherokee tale suggests that we have within us two natures—the good wolf and the evil wolf, and we make a choice—with every thought, word and action as to which one we feed.

The challenge of the spiritual life is to *choose* to remain aligned with the Word within in all our thoughts, words and deeds so that eventually our awareness will naturally "sit" with the Word within rather than aligning with ego. Our goal is to develop this capacity to such an extent that our awareness of the Word within becomes the "default" consciousness governing our thoughts, words and deeds rather than allowing the insatiable desires and cravings of the ego to be our driving force and definitive default setting influencing how we relate to God, one another, the world around us and life itself.

Cultivating our awareness of the Word within reveals that we and all of creation are intrinsically interconnected, one body with many parts. Jesus, it seems, lived his life from this perspective. He was grounded in the truth that we are first and foremost children of God and as such we are absolutely connected to and part of an evolving universe whose origins are rooted in a common beginning. All things came forth from the mouth of God. We and all creation came forth as God's Word!

When we hold this as the ultimate reality, we see that all things are united as the Word of God and that all creation is an expression of the divine. This perception points us to the larger context of our common beginnings. That is, we realize that the source and sustenance of life, regardless of what we call it or how we describe it, is the same for all of us and all of creation. From this vantage point, we can no longer deny the sacredness of life or the sanctity of relationships, whether mundane or supernatural. When we live in conscious awareness of our union with God, we live attuned to the Word within and touch upon the truth that underlies Jesus' very life and ministry—that we are one.

Saint Paul articulates this concept most clearly when he describes Christians as members of the mystical body of Christ. We are each unique; we each have a different function, different flaws and talents, but none of us is replaceable. The church needs all of us.

OUR SOURCE AND SUSTENANCE

A Samaritan woman came to draw water, and Jesus said to her, "Give me a drink." (His disciples had gone to the city to buy food.) The Samaritan woman said to him, "How is it that you, a Jew, ask a drink of me, a woman of Samaria?" (Jews do not share things in common with Samaritans.) Jesus answered her, "If you knew the gift of God, and who it is that is saying to you, 'Give me a drink,' you would have asked him, and he would have given you living water." The woman said to him, "Sir, you have no bucket, and the well is deep. Where do you get that living water? Are you greater than our ancestor Jacob, who gave us the well, and with his sons and his flocks drank from it?" Jesus said to her, "Everyone who drinks of this water will be thirsty again, but those who drink of the water that I will give them will never be thirsty. The water that I will give will become in them a spring of water gushing up to eternal life." The woman said to him, "Sir, give me this water, so that I may never be thirsty or have to keep coming here to draw water." (John 4:7–15)

As in any relationship, our relationship with God demands something of us. If we are going to take seriously our responsibility in cultivating this relationship, we must give it time, energy and attention. By engaging in the practice of prayer and contemplation, we stimulate and reawaken our connection with God. Spiritual practice is a tool that helps us return to the ground of all being, the Word of God, from which all creation springs. The aim of spiritual practice is to discover that we have never been, nor could we ever be, separate from God or separate from one other. All life, all creation, and even our very breath are dependent on God, our source and our sustenance.

Returning our awareness to the source and sustenance of all creation, the Word of God, is the essence of prayer. Developing a spiritual practice of prayer and contemplation helps extend our awareness of God's presence with us so that our dependence on God is not only evident in our prayer time, but throughout our day, during all times and in all circumstances. Eventually, with practice, we will find that we are so firmly grounded in the Word within, and awareness of our union with God is so strong, we can stand in the face of fire and not be consumed.

The "fires" we face can be anything from self-criticism or criticism by others, self-doubt, damage to our reputations, an over-whelming experience of loss or despair or any kind of negativity that attempts to distract us from the truth that we are made in the image and likeness of God. At times the fires of life can be so fierce and all-consuming that we may feel that God has com-pletely abandoned us. We may feel as if we have lost contact with God. Whatever the "fire," regardless of how great its intensity, prayer helps us face it in confidence that God makes all things work together for the good.

Prayer brings us again and again into the presence of God. In the story of Jesus and the Samaritan woman, Jesus refers to the source and sustenance of all life as "living water." This water has an immortal, ever-enduring and inextinguishable quality to it. This "living water" is always available to us even though we can ignore it or suppress it. We can allow our thoughts, opinions and circumstances to grow so loud and heavy that we can no longer hear the spring of living water trickling deep within us. We can become so consumed by the demands of the roles we play that we become like the Samaritan woman, unaware that this "living water" is within our grasp, searching instead for sat-isfaction in extraneous activities, material possessions and fleet-ing relationships.

"Everyone who drinks this water [from Jacob's well] will be thirsty again, but whoever drinks the water I will give will never thirst again." Trying to find our purpose and potential in external things will never fully satisfy us. We will be thirsty again. On the contrary, when we draw from the spring of living water, which is synonymous with returning to the Word within, we find not only our source and our sustenance, but also the means by which we can be led to our purpose and potential.

Prayer and contemplation are the conduits through which we draw from the well of living water, and make contact with the Word within. Spending time in prayer and contemplation is like bathing in our union with God. By developing a steadfast practice of prayer and contemplation we can be cleansed of our egotisti cal impulses and selfish desires and begin again to align ourselves with God's desire for us.

PRACTICE

Ego Identification Practice

Sit silently for ten minutes. Try not to move your body. Simply observe your thoughts as they arise. Do not resist them. Do not entertain or engage them. Do not judge them or identify yourself with them. Simply watch them. When you find that you have followed or engaged a thought, let it go. Release it. Continue to keep your body still, quiet your mind and begin observing again the thoughts that arise in your mind. Do this for ten to twenty minutes every morning and before bedtime, if possible. This exercise helps us begin to develop an awareness of how and when our minds are controlled by thought. Developing the capacity to observe our thoughts, actions and reactions is the key to recognizing when and how we are under the influence of ego.

Contemplation

Read the entire text containing the shema, Deuteronomy 6:4−9. Memorize the first line: "Hear, O Israel: The LORD is our God, the LORD alone." Say it upon waking up in the morning, prior to meals and just before you go to sleep for the night. After a week of this practice, reflect on how this action has affected your daily consciousness.

Consider how your life's journey compares with that of the Israelites from Egypt to the Promised Land. When have you had to let go of the known to enter the wilderness of the unknown? How did you survive or endure this transition?

Prayer

Loving God, Divine Oneness, open my heart, mind and being to the unity of all life. Help me to see and hear your Word in myself, my neighbor, in all my relationships and all of creation. Let the Word open in me like a lotus so that the Christ consciousness may find expression through me. Amen.

Action of Loving-kindness

This week look for someone who displays the Christ consciousness. Drop them a note or an e-mail and let them know you noticed their generous spirit, courage, kindness or compassion.

CHAPTER TWO

WAKE UP!

But about that day or hour no one knows, neither the angels in heaven, nor the Son, but only the Father. Beware, keep alert; for you do not know when the time will come. It is like a man going on a journey, when he leaves home and puts his slaves in charge, each with his work, and commands the doorkeeper to be on the watch. Therefore, keep awake—for you do not know when the master of the house will come, in the evening, or at midnight, or at cockcrow, or at dawn, or else he may find you asleep when he comes suddenly. And what I say to you I say to all: Keep awake. (Mark 13:32–37)

We live in a universe that is constantly expanding, evolving and emerging. This dynamic flow can be seen as the process of connecting, where "things," "people" and even "personalities" come into temporary existence because of and through relationships. Nothing exists independent of relationships. Nothing. Not God—our understanding of the trinity makes that clear. Not you and me. Not the planet we live on or the cosmos of which we are a part. Relationships are the web of life underlying all creation. Jesus' life reflected this.

Jesus proclaimed the importance of relationship every time he stood up for the oppressed, the poor, the abandoned and outcast. He recognized that if one of us is hungry, it reveals a hunger in all of us. If one of us is diseased, we all experience disease. If one of us in not included, we are not whole. This is why he healed the wounded, fed the hungry and challenged any abuse of power. This is why he commanded us to love our enemies. This is why he invited everyone to the table—everyone! Women, tax collectors, zealots and sinners!

Jesus drew near those most easily dismissed because he was so strongly convinced that nothing separated him from them and nothing separated them from God. Nothing and no one is separate from the rest. We are interconnected to each other and to God.

What we do to our enemy, we do to ourselves. When we fail to reach out to another, when we fail to uplift another, we bury ourselves. Until we see ourselves and all creation as one, as an intimately connected body of Christ, we fail to envision the kingdom for which Jesus gave his life and we miss entirely the reason for gathering together to pray and break bread in community.

We are immersed in relationships and if we desire to follow the path of Jesus we have to develop the capacity to see God in ourselves and others—*all* others, at *all* times. Developing this capacity requires that we trust that the Word within is contained in each person, circumstance or relationship with which we are involved. An even greater challenge is to remain convinced of this when that is not immediately apparent. Responding and relating to the deeper truth, regardless of what a given situation presents, opens the door to manifesting the Christ consciousness in ourselves and calling it forth in others.

Our relationship with God is like any other relationship. If we open ourselves and allow ourselves to be exposed to the presence and power of God, we will be changed by it. Our relationship with God has to be nurtured so that as we grow, it grows, as we change it changes and as it blossoms, we blossom into the person we are called to be. If our relationship with God has not changed over the years, if we are still praying in the same way we prayed as children—or if we have quit praying altogether—if our image of God is still an old man with a white beard, we can be sure that our relationship with God has grown stale and stagnant. By grounding ourselves in the Word of God through prayer, cultivating the ability to be still in mind and body, and listening for God, we discover that in our relationship with God we have a trustworthy friend who is closer to us than our own breath.

Friends are those who choose to accompany us through the ups and downs of life. Those who stay with us as we journey through the joys and sorrows, dry deserts and fertile valleys are companions who make a difference in our lives. Friendship gives us opportunities to safely discover and test our limits and evolve as our life unfolds. God alone makes the entire journey with us.

God alone is with us prior to our conception and beyond our death. God alone knit us in our mother's womb. God alone knows the secrets we carry, the dreams we hold, the doubts we have and the challenges we face. God alone is our constant companion, our beloved and our friend. This is the relationship that must be primary in our lives if we truly desire to discover lasting contentment, purpose and meaning.

God uses everything to communicate with us. Nothing is beneath being an opening for God. The sacred Scriptures are one means of communication, but nature, relationships, music, art, stars and birds, babes and sages awaken us to the beauty before us, guide our lives and draw us into deeper awareness of our communion with God and the Word contained in all creation.

Deepening our awareness of God's presence in our lives is critical to nurturing this relationship. Jesus advises us all to "Keep awake." Rumi, the great Sufi mystic and poet from the thirteenth century, who often referred to God as "the Friend," once said when speaking of our relationship with the divine, "Our friendship is made of being awake."[1]

Jesus' challenge to keep awake summons us to develop a keen sense of God's presence. It demands that we be perpetually open to the possibility that God's presence can be found in everything, every circumstance, every relationship and all creation. The call to stay awake implies that God can use absolutely any relationship, circumstance or encounter as an opening, as a means of communication or revelation. If we want to nurture our relationship with God and resonate with the Word within, we have to begin to look and listen for God in every moment—in the ordinary and mundane as well as the special and sacred moments of our lives. Awakening to God's presence in the moment can come through conversation with a friend, an encounter with a stranger or simply in meeting the eyes of someone who needs to be seen.

Awakening involves developing the ability to see that all things, people and creation are interconnected by the Maker's design. God's presence is in the beauty of the green Earth, the blue water of the rivers and oceans, and in the deep black space of the heavens. The presence of God is in the eyes of a child, in the wisdom of one who has weathered what comes through the ages, and even in those who remain forgotten on the fringes of society. All of creation is imbued with the love of God and thus has the potential to reveal God's love to us.

As Rumi indicated, this friendship relies on our being awake to it, aware of it. However, for most of us awakening is not a one-time occurrence. It is something we have to do over and over because keeping awake is about growing in consciousness, growing in awareness of God's presence in all things, at all times. While growth of any kind can be difficult because it may demand that we change our perspective, do things differently or make different choices, developing a spiritual practice can assist us in this transformation.

Our spiritual practice will only bear fruit if we put our relationship with God first. Prayer and contemplation are the portals through which communication flows, intimacy grows and a sense of the interconnectedness of all things arises, but putting our relationship with God first demands that we return time and time again to such practices—whether or not we are able to discern the fruit of our labors.

Consistently engaging in spiritual practices such as prayer, contemplation and acts of loving-kindness are the antidotes for sleepwalking through life, but staying awake takes more than spiritual practice. It takes commitment to maintaining the primacy of this relationship with God. It means choosing God as our Beloved and Friend. Developing this kind of relationship with God requires regularly turning to God for counsel and listening for God's Word in our hearts. In this way, the Word of God becomes the rudder that steers us to our destiny and points us in the direction of our life's purpose.

MAKING AN EFFORT

...When it was evening, the disciples came to him and said, "This is a deserted place, and the hour is now late; send the crowds away so that they may go into the villages and buy food for themselves." Jesus said to them, "They need not go away; you give them something to eat." They replied, "We have nothing here but five loaves and two fish." And he said, "Bring them here to me." Then he ordered the crowds to sit down on the grass. Taking the five loaves and the two fish, he looked up to heaven, and blessed and broke the loaves, and gave them to the disciples, and the disciples gave them to the crowds. And all ate and were filled; and they took up what was left over of the broken pieces, twelve baskets full. And those who ate were about five thousand men, besides women and children.

> Immediately he made the disciples get into the boat and go
> on ahead to the other side, while he dismissed the crowds. And
> after he had dismissed the crowds, he went up the mountain by
> himself to pray. (Matthew 14:15–23)

According to Sister Joan Chittister, O.S.B., "Prayer is what forms us in the presence of God. To fail to do it formally and regularly is to barter the only relationship in life that is guaranteed."[2] Cultivating a prayer practice is crucial to nurturing our relationship with God because prayer pulls us out of preoccupation with ourselves. In prayer, we lift our mind and heart to God and begin to see that our seemingly solitary lives are connected to all life, that ultimately there is only one life in which we all partake.

If we desire to keep God as our Beloved and Friend, we must pray. The essence of prayer is returning. Returning again and again to God's Word in the Scriptures, in nature, in ourselves and in others. Returning to silence and stillness. Returning to the heart where our deepest center is located and arousing our deepest self in the presence of God.

Prayer is our response to the often silent but persistent desire to become what we are really meant to be. Calling out to God is a response to the Word within. It is a response to the Word that has already been placed in our mouths and in our hearts. The act of prayer brings God's goodness to us in the same way an infant's cry causes milk to flow from her mother's breast. The response is immediate and certain. God waits to nourish us in prayer.

When we pray, we make ourselves aware of God's presence and express the intimacy we share with one who knows us completely. We acknowledge that we, all of nature and the cosmos are hemmed in by God. God surrounds us on all sides.

We have to set aside time to be with God alone. Like Jesus, we too have to "go up the mountain to pray." We have to leave the busy activities of the day and take time to meet God in the silence of our hearts. We have to be willing to remove ourselves from the things that distract us from God's presence in our lives so we can more fully give our heart, mind and spirit to God.

"Going up the mountain to pray" as Jesus did, implies a substantial effort. We don't have to literally climb a mountain, but for those of us with busy schedules setting aside time, regularly, to be alone with God, might seem even more insurmountable. Running a mile one day won't restore your cardiovascular system, but running a mile every day might. Spending a few moments in prayer one day won't change your life, but spending a few moments in prayer every day might.

Praying allows us to give voice to our deepest desires, our greatest fears and our most daring hopes. Returning to the practice even when we are unable to discern God's presence is essential to maintaining the steadfast perseverance this relationship requires if we are truly going to allow it to transform us. Developing an innate trust that the Word is contained in our flesh, that you and I are made in the image and likeness of God regardless of how we appear, present ourselves or come off to others, is the payoff prayer offers.

Developing that kind of trust in the one who created us frees us to try new things. It frees us to fail, to make mistakes, because we know that no matter what, we have the Word within; we belong to God. Nothing changes that. Not the gravest of sins, number of failures or losses. Getting to that level of trust depends on believing that nothing can separate us from God.

Engaging in a regular prayer practice can support us through the changes and challenges of life, and comfort us in times of doubt and distress, but we have to be willing to make an effort, to persevere even when prayer becomes difficult. Returning to the Word within, trusting that it is the essence of our being, even when we cannot sense it is there, is how we make it through the deserts of doubt and despair that the journey of transformation involves.

A HOME FOR GOD

> Judas said to him, "Lord, how is it that you will reveal yourself to us, and not to the world?" Jesus answered him, "Those who love me will keep my word, and my Father will love them, and we will come to them and make our home with them. Whoever does not love me does not keep my words; and the word that you hear is not mine, but is from the Father who sent me."
> (John 14:22–24)

There are many ways to pray. Explore different methods of prayer and meditation from both Eastern and Western spiritual traditions. Find what works best for you. One means of discovering the Word within is centering prayer.

In *New Seeds of Contemplation*, Thomas Merton wrote,

> God utters me like a word containing a partial thought of Himself. A word will never be able to comprehend the voice that utters it. But if I am true to the concept that God utters in me, if I am true to thought of Him I was meant to embody, I

shall be full of His actuality and find Him everywhere in myself, and find myself nowhere. I shall be lost in Him.[3]

If, like Merton, we desire to remain true to the Word of God uttered in us, committing to a steadfast practice of prayer is essential. Centering prayer helps us not only access the Word within, but it also assists us in growing into the Word of God we are meant to embody and express in the world.

Centering prayer allows us to enter into communication and foster intimacy in our relationship with God. It helps us discover that indeed we are the Word of God en-fleshed, that the Word of God is contained in all creation, and as a result, all of creation gives expression to God. Centering prayer connects us to God and deepens our understanding. It can lead us to the well of union where our greatest potential lies and can help us grow into the person God desires us to be.

Though centering prayer is an ancient Christian prayer form, it can still be used today as a relevant and reliable means to cultivating an intimate relationship with God.

According to M. Basil Pennington, author of *Centering Prayer: Renewing an Ancient Christian Prayer Form*, there are three simple rules guiding the practice of centering prayer. They are:

> Take a minute or two to quiet both mind and body and bring oneself into awareness of God's presence dwelling in our depths; also upon completion of the prayer take several minutes to come out, mentally praying the Lord's Prayer or some other prayer.
>
> After resting for a bit in the presence of God, take up a simple word that expresses this response and begin to let it repeat itself within.

Whenever in the course of prayer we become aware of anything else, simply gently return to the Presence by use of the
prayer word.[4]

Let us spend some time with each of these rules in order to better understand how to engage in this practice.

Begin by relaxing as deeply as possible, quieting your mind
and body. The mind remains alert and awake, aware of everything, but focused on nothing. As you let go more and more, you
are doing physically what you also desire to do mentally—letting
go and resting in God.

Letting go and resting in God begins by cultivating a posture of
loving attentiveness to the fact that God is the source and sustenance of all life. Gently recognize that everything is held in and
contained in God. The psalmist expresses this consciousness by
saying, "You hem me in, behind and before, / and lay your hand
upon me" (Psalm 139:5). This is the awareness you are trying to
cultivate as you descend, both body and mind, into stillness.

After resting in the stillness, centering prayer begins with *lectio,*
or what Pennington refers to as "an instantaneous recall of the
goodness of God's creative and redeeming love" and then moves
into *meditatio* or "momentary reflection" on God's goodness,
which evokes *oratio,* or a "response of faith-full love, which brings
us into the Presence" which in turn readies us for *contemplatio,* "to
simply *be* to that wonderful Presence."[5]

Quieting your body and mind and bringing yourself into the
awareness of the presence of God should take a few minutes at
most. This resting place gives way to a prayer of quiet recollection,
of presence. This is the heart of centering prayer. It is an attempt

to tune in, or align ourselves with the Word within. Here, in this presence, we strive to stay alert and awake to this presence alone.

The purpose of the second guideline—taking up and gently repeating a prayer word—is to facilitate your ability to remain in this presence. Gently recalling and repeating this simple prayer word when you realize you have been distracted returns your attention to God's presence. The prayer word you choose should be an expression of God's steadfast love. Many choose the name of Jesus as their prayer word. Others use a word such as *Abba* (Father), *Amma* (Mother) or *Sophia* (wisdom). Still others choose a short phrase such as "letting go" or "God alone" as an expression of their relationship with God.

Centering prayer does not consist of repeating the prayer word continuously. Rather, it should easily rest in your heart and whenever you find that you have been distracted by engaging a thought, feeling or emotion, gently employ the prayer word to fully return your attention to God's presence. Thoughts and feelings will come and go as you seek to remain in a constant state of awareness of God's presence. The challenge is not to rid yourself of thoughts and feelings, but to disengage from entertaining them. When you realize you have been lost in thought or distracted by a feeling or emotion and your attention has drifted away from the Beloved, your Friend, invoke your prayer word to gently return your attention to this loving presence that constantly surrounds you and desires to make a home in you.

After twenty minutes or so, bring some of this depth of attention to God back with you to your everyday activities of living. In order to do so, you need to bring your attention back from the

depths of silence and stillness and gently prepare yourself to perceive the presence of God in all aspects of your life and relationships. This kind of practice is how the Word within germinates
and begins to take root in us.

Becoming a dwelling place for God begins with our commitment—our commitment to becoming, our commitment to transformation. Our commitment to free ourselves from our egos
places us directly on the path of Jesus.

Bringing our awareness to God's presence through centering
prayer is just the beginning of keeping God's Word. Cultivating
this relationship requires returning again and again to the Word
within. By investing ourselves in and making our relationship with
God the primary relationship of our lives, we begin our transformation from simply housing the Word of God to becoming a
home, a dwelling place and full-blown expression of God's unity.

P RACTICE

Ego Identification Exercise

Take some time at the end of the day and do a review. Look over
your entire day, your interactions and your attitude. Identify
when you were acting from the perspective of the ego. In order
to see the ego at play, look for overreactions, defensiveness or
self-pity. Do not judge yourself when you see that you've been
acting out of ego: simply acknowledge it. Then, in your mind,
replay the interaction. As you replay the interaction, imagine
how you would have responded if you were planted securely in
the Word within. Really consider the difference between the two
scenarios—reacting from ego and reacting from the Word within,
that place deep within where we know we are one with God.

Contemplation

Jesus said, "Those who love me will keep my word, and [God] will love them, and we will come to them and make our home with them" (John 14:23). What does it mean to you "to keep God's word?" How do you or how can you prepare yourself to be a home for God?

Prayer

Reread "A Home for God" (on page 35) and follow the directions for engaging in centering prayer.

Action of Loving-kindness

Share a meal with someone who is going through a difficult time. Do not try to solve their problem. Instead, offer your presence to them by actively listening or simply being with them.

CHAPTER THREE

UNLEASHING THE CHRIST CONSCIOUSNESS

I will not leave you orphaned; I am coming to you. In a little while the world will no longer see me, but you will see me; because I live, you also will live. On that day you will know that I am in my Father, and you in me, and I in you. They who have my commandments and keep them are those who love me; and those who love me will be loved by my Father, and I will love them and reveal myself to them. (John 14:18–21)

Change is difficult. It is rarely something we enter into willingly or eagerly. Yet, it is the only way we can realize the Word within and grow into the person God made us to be. Transformation is the only means through which the Word within can be brought forth and manifest as the Christ consciousness in the world. Change through choice is the only fertilizer for this seed.

Meister Eckhart, a Dominican mystic from the Middle Ages, said, "The seed of a pear tree grows into a pear tree; and a hazel seed grows into a hazel tree; a seed of God grows into God."[1] The "seed" he's referring to is the Word of God contained in us and all creation. Eckhart reminds us that we have been made in the image and likeness of God. This is the foundation upon which we were conceived. This is our essence. To become like God, to become Christlike—this is our destiny.

The words of Jesus from John's Gospel, "I am in [God] and you are in me and I am in you," challenge us to live with a heightened awareness of the presence of God. The vocation of our lives is to live in this seamless union with God and allow our lives to be an expression of trust in this union. The path of Jesus, if we take it up ourselves, can lead us to deep trust in our union with God. Ultimately, this union, if we come to rely on it, can unearth our greatest potential and bring us to our destiny.

However, following the path of Jesus is not just about being good people. Our goal is not just to be good. It's to become like God, to become Christlike in our thoughts, words and deeds. For most of us, the majority of our life is spent establishing our individual identity, developing those skills, characteristics and tendencies that make us stand out, or set us apart from the crowd. While this is necessary to some degree for an individual's healthy development, we have made it the apex of what it means to be human. And this is where we miss the mark.

The life of Jesus reveals that the height of humanity can only be reached by striving for divinity, by striving to become like God. Becoming like God is expressed as our own ability to create goodness by bringing life out of death, light of out darkness, abundance from scarcity, comfort to the diseased and healing to the wounded. The degree to which we become sharing beings— sharing both ourselves and our possessions—reveals the degree to which we are becoming like God.

This desire to become like God, lived out in our lives, through our relationships, the work we do and the way that we do it, is the Word within manifesting as the Christ consciousness in the world. The impulse to grow and change and experience new ways of thinking and being, this is the presence of Jesus alive in our hearts! The desire to be a better person, to grow in love, compassion and forgiveness is the Word within urging us to grow into the likeness of God for which we have been created. When we actually engage in forgiveness, compassion and love, it is the Christ consciousness breaking through our lives.

We can be sure that the Christ consciousness is emerging through us when we are able to see ourselves in another, to put ourselves in another's shoes and as a result, reach out to them, forgive them and welcome them into our hearts. When our passion to grow and be engaged—really engaged—in this life is stronger and deeper than our desire to simply subsist and get by, it is the Christ consciousness groaning and pleading to be manifested through us and released into the world.

On the contrary, we have also known that part of ourselves that resists change and transformation. This is the voice that says, "Why bother?" or "Put it off until tomorrow," or, "There's no use in trying, I'm never going to change." This is our ego talking. For most of us, the ego may be the only voice we ever hear. It often gets all or most of our attention. It is the voice that seems to come out of nowhere and encourage us to sabotage any real effort of pursuing lasting transformation. It manifests in our lives as lethargy, laziness and self-loathing. It is the drive that lures us to comfort rather than conversion, accepts mediocrity rather than pursuing excellence, and prefers ambiguity to transparency.

If transformation is the task of our lives, then we have to face our ego and take on the challenge to change our relationship with it and the way we allow it to influence us. Think about the goal of competition. We say we compete to win. But is that really the goal?

We participate in competition, not just to win, but to become better players ourselves. By taking on an opponent or adversary we develop strength and skill. The possibility or experience of losing ignites a deeper desire in us to improve our abilities. As we develop we begin to understand that the game challenges us on a multitude of levels. While it may require that we develop physically, it may also require that we grow emotionally, psychologically and intellectually as well. In order to defeat our opponent we have to consider the strategy they will employ and the strengths they bring to the fight. The same goes for our relationship with ego.

In order to do that, we have to learn how to observe our ego nature without judgment. By increasing our awareness of our ego we can begin to identify when we are acting out of it. Once we are able to discern the nature and influence of our ego, we can consciously begin to unhook ourselves from it while strengthening our resolve to resist the lure of our egotistical desires.

Still, sometimes it seems as though we are programmed to fail when it comes to improving the quality of our lives and our relationship with God. The desires generated from our ego constantly pull at us and attempt to influence and control our behavior, sabotaging our good intentions and deflating our excitement and eagerness to change. Adding to the difficulty is the fact that most of us, when given an option of which path to take, choose the path of least resistance. Most often, that path is the path of the ego.

In our discomfort and discontent we often look for the easy way out of challenging circumstances and distance ourselves from relationships that try us and test us. We look for the people, places and situations in which we feel most at ease, but staying comfortable does not lend itself to transformation. Jesus' life affirms that if we want to follow in his footsteps on the journey to becoming, if we want to bring forth the Christ consciousness in our lives and bring it to bear on the world in which we live, we cannot expect to remain comfortable.

Jesus did not shrink from the challenges of his day, nor did he hide from the uncomfortable or unpleasant. He confronted poverty and injustice of all kinds. He gave his life to those people and situations that demanded his compassion and his strength. He showed us that we too have to confront those things we would rather deny, look straight at the disease from which we would rather turn away, and move into those areas of our lives that feel uncomfortable so that we can be transformed by them. Rumi said it this way:

> An empty mirror and your worst destructive habits, when they are held up to each other, that's when the real making begins. That's what art and crafting are. A tailor needs a torn garment to practice his expertise. Your doctor must have a broken leg to doctor. Your defects are the way that glory gets manifested. Whoever sees clearly what is diseased in himself begins to gallop on the way.[2]

Transformation is the purpose of our lives—to change and be changed until the Christ consciousness is fully developed and the ego sufficiently starved so that it becomes too weak to influence our behavior and choices. Every time we change or are changed for the better, every time we grow in wisdom and understanding, strength and loving-kindness, the presence of Jesus comes to the fore in us. And instead of meeting the world with our eyes, suddenly our eyes are opened and we see others and the world around us through the eyes of Jesus. This is how the Word within manifests itself as the Christ consciousness in the world.

Like Jesus, we are called to give absolutely everything of ourselves to this task, to this transformation. With every thought, word and deed, we must ask ourselves if we are moving nearer to becoming like God, nearer to aligning with the Word within, or if we are moving further away from that potential. The spiritual path cannot be trod, nor the goal of union with God attained by those of us who "sort of" desire it. Half-heartedness will not get us to our destination. Becoming an unobstructed vessel through which the Christ consciousness can flow into our lives, our relationships and the world takes profound perseverance and unwavering commitment to spiritual practice.

SINGLE-MINDEDNESS

> Now as they went on their way, he entered a certain village, where a woman named Martha welcomed him into her home. She had a sister named Mary, who sat at the Lord's feet and listened to what he was saying. But Martha was distracted by her many tasks; so she came to him and asked, "Lord, do you not care that my sister has left me to do all the work by myself? Tell her then to help me." But the Lord answered her, "Martha, Martha, you are worried and distracted by many things; there is need of only one thing. Mary has chosen the better part, which will not be taken away from her." (Luke 10:38–42)

Thomas Merton, in *New Seeds of Contemplation*, described contemplation as:

> ...the response to a call: a call from the [One] Who has no voice, and yet Who speaks in everything that is, and Who, most of all speaks in the depths of our own being: for we ourselves are words of [God]. We are words that are meant to respond to [God], to answer to [God], to echo [God] and even in·some way to contain [God] and signify [God]. Contemplation is this echo. It is a deep resonance in the inmost center of our spirit in which our very life loses its separate voice and re-sounds with the majesty and the mercy of the Hidden and Living One.[3]

Contemplation, like centering prayer, is a channel of communication through which we join ourselves to the Word of God

concealed and alive in ourselves and in all creation. Such practices provide fertile soil in which the Word within can germinate,
sink deep roots and grow into the fullest expression of God it is
intended to convey through us.

We are words that are meant to respond to God! There is no
greater meaning to derive from life than freely and fully giving
ourselves to God, to the greater good of humanity and all creation. That does not mean we have to have a great deal of money,
prestige or renown. Rather, it means really engaging in the life we
have been given. It means taking complete responsibility for our
physical, emotional, intellectual and spiritual growth. It means
taking responsibility for the degree of contentment and discontent we experience in our lives.

Giving ourselves to God and the greater good of all does not
require grandiose gestures. It *does* require doing small things with
great love. It means wholeheartedly committing to seeing the
presence of God in all others, as well as ourselves. It means ready-
ing ourselves to see God in the very next person we greet. In order
to do that, we may be required to let go of our conditioned
responses and prejudices. It may require us to step out of our
"normal" or accepted roles and refuse injustice regardless of the
cost to us. This is exactly what Mary does in this Gospel passage.

In this passage we find Mary sitting at the feet of Jesus. This, it
should be noted, was a place usually reserved for men because it
implies that one is a student, and being a student, in those days,
was reserved for a teacher's disciples, who were exclusively male.
Mary's placement at Jesus' feet is an indication that she is free—
free from the fear of rejection, and free from the obligation to

maintain a role that has been carved out for her by men. Mary's commitment to freedom is revealed in her determination to cultivate her relationship with Jesus, no matter what accepted roles and cultural norms must be transcended in order to do so.

Like Mary, first and foremost, we have to attend to and respond to the Word in our midst. However, the decision to make the Word within the center of our attention is one that must be made *freely*. Real companionship between ourselves and God cannot be forged out of feelings of obligation, fear or guilt. Mary's place at Jesus' feet tells us that unless we come to this relationship from a pure desire to be the person God calls us to be, and unless we remain radically open to the possibility that the accepted idea of what this relationship is supposed to look like according to the religious institutions and accepted traditions of the day may be something different than it actually is, we may find ourselves committed to an institution rather than Jesus.

Following in Jesus' footsteps requires us to be single-minded about the pursuit of freedom, liberation and truth at all costs. For most of us it is easy to say that we are committed to these values, but freedom, liberation and truth, from the perspective of Jesus and pursuing the spiritual path, have a radically different meaning than when these values are placed in a military or imperialist context. Pursuing freedom in a spiritual context calls us to distinguish in *ourselves* the desire to be free, to grow, change and evolve in consciousness versus the desire to be enslaved, maintain the status quo, stay comfortable and live every day like the rest, passing the years of our lives in mundane mediocrity.

In order to discern this, we have to be willing to reflect on our experiences and our reactions to them. We have to learn how to scrutinize our responses and reactions so we can become aware of what beliefs, assumptions or conditioned habits are motivating and influencing us. In this way, we begin to discern if and when our actions and reactions are aligned with the Word within. Selflessness, mutuality and nonviolence expressed in our thoughts, words and deeds are the fruits born from aligning our actions with the Word within. As a result, the Christ consciousness flows through us unhindered and acts as salve for our wounded world.

Committing to the path of growth, change and evolution is the path of Jesus. Consciously stepping out on the path of transformation, while remaining rooted in the Word within, is an effective way to restrict the influence of our ego-driven patterns on our behavior and in our thinking so we can get out of the way and allow the actualization of the Christ consciousness to come through us.

One of the sure signs that our ego is at work is the drive or inclination to maintain the status quo and to stay comfortable. Resisting change and aspiring to nothing more than mediocrity is the way we become enslaved to ego. It is the voice of the ego that says, "Oh it can wait until tomorrow," or, "I know I said I was going to take better care of myself through diet and exercise, but what is one more day and another bowl of ice cream?" It's the ego that says, "It can wait" or "I'm doing well enough. There is no need for me to change."

Admitting that we are still enslaved by cultural norms, middle-class values and material possessions that give us a false sense of security is how we begin to push aside our ego desires and make room for the Christ consciousness to rise up in us. If we want to unleash the Christ consciousness and bring it forth into the world, we have to cultivate our desire for transformation by becoming more like Mary. Like Mary, we must challenge the norms, attitudes and prejudices that keep our minds enslaved and our hearts closed.

All slavery, subtle or obvious, originates from the unquenchable desire of the ego to get its needs met. Narcissism, greed, self-consumption and an unfounded belief that one life has greater value than another originate from an inability to resist the cravings of the ego. The ego is always vying for survival at the cost of others, and even at a deep cost to ourselves. Only when we begin to see where we are chained, how we withhold from being fully engaged in life, and why we participate in that disempowerment will we be moved to change it.

The demands of this commitment to freedom are difficult to confront because it means we have to desire to express the Christ consciousness more than we desire to be liked. We have to desire freedom from ego more than we desire to be successful. We have to want to realize greater consciousness more than we want to be wealthy, renowned or recognized. And most of us are not willing to do that.

Yet, if we want the Word within to be unleashed as the Christ consciousness in the world, we have to desire to stay on the path of Jesus more than pursuing anything else. If we are serious about pursuing the path of Jesus, it requires that we acknowledge that there are relationships, roles and other things in our lives that we treasure more than we treasure the idea of expressing the Word within as the Christ consciousness in the world. The reason it is important to acknowledge the allure such things can have for us is because we cannot change what we do not acknowledge.

A direct approach is to call to mind the object of your love and longing and while holding a picture of this person, place or thing in your mind, say "not mine." You will be able to feel the tug on your heart for those things to which your identity is attached. It is good to engage in this kind of contemplation regularly if we want to unleash the Christ consciousness because only when we realize that those things do not make us who we are do we begin to understand who we really are and to whom we really belong.

The challenge of taking up the path of Jesus is to recognize that if we want to be free to be the person God created us to be, if we want to unleash the Christ consciousness, we have to be willing to go against the norm, against the "way things have always been done." We have to begin making choices from the viewpoint of the Christ consciousness, in which the unity of all things is apparent, rather than making choices from the perspective of self-consciousness, in which we perceive ourselves as separate from God, others and the rest of creation.

Allowing our lives to be a channel through which the Christ consciousness is unleashed in the world is a consequence of recognizing that we are answerable to God alone for the way we spend our lives, and for the ways we are complicit in our own complacency. Chances are if we are always doing the expected, we are not manifesting the Christ consciousness in the world. And frankly, this is what we have to do if we are to live the prophetic and powerful lives we are called to live.

What was Jesus saying, when he said to Martha, "there is need of only one thing" in response to her concern over her sister's behavior? What if that "one thing" to be concerned about and consumed with was cultivating a desire to be free? What if we put the desire to actualize the Christ consciousness at the center of our spirituality? Even more, at the center of our entire lives?

When we truly cultivate a desire to be free, we begin to distance ourselves from the things that prohibit us from manifesting the Christ consciousness. We begin to see and understand that this is it! This is everything right now! Right here! We cannot keep putting off until tomorrow what we know we need to do today.

Cultivating the ability to actualize the Christ consciousness forces us to examine the purity of our intentions and motivations. When we do that with complete honesty, we begin to recognize that our motivations usually are not so pure. In fact, fear runs much of our lives by encouraging us to keep the status quo. Consequently we end up choosing to live monotonous, untried and untested lives that constrict our humanity.

In this Gospel story, Mary tests the waters of freedom, by not doing the expected, by stepping out of the "acceptable," and into the Christ consciousness rather than her ego. By her actions Mary reveals that she knows that first and foremost she is called to be attentive to Jesus' presence—the Word of God—in her midst, rather than strictly doing what is expected of her. This is courage. This is freedom. This is how the Christ consciousness is birthed into the world.

Indeed, this Gospel passage challenges all of us to discern what the "one thing" is to which Jesus refers when he says, "There is need of only one thing." Think about how the world would be different if each one of us gave our lives to cultivating a desire to be free from ego, free from self-consumption, free from endless self-concern. What if unleashing the Christ consciousness in the world was the fundamental motivation of our lives? Maybe then we would understand Jesus' urgency to pursue the kingdom.

If unleashing the Christ consciousness was the primary motivating force in our lives, we would make decisions based on what would benefit the whole rather than basing our decisions on what benefits us as individuals. We would pursue justice, equality and mutuality at all costs because we would realize that in order for the kingdom to come, it must come through us for all of us.

Jesus' words, "There is need of only one thing," challenge us to break out of the chains of complacency and commitment to comfort and pursue the one thing, the only thing that is necessary to taking up the path of Jesus—freedom. The desire to be free above all else is a mark of the holy. So we must ask ourselves: How are we not yet free? How are we complacent and complicit in our own slavery? How do we contribute to the constriction of others' abilities to manifest the Christ consciousness? What does Mary's seemingly small act of disobedience tell us about pursuing freedom from ego and engaging the path of Jesus?

More than ever we have to take conscious steps toward the *one thing*, toward freedom from ego so that we can freely give ourselves to the lives—the significant lives—God put us on the planet to lead.

All for One and One for All

For just as the body is one and has many members, and all the members of the body, though many, are one body, so it is with Christ. For in the one Spirit we were all baptized into one body—Jews or Greeks, slaves or free—and we were all made to drink of one Spirit.

Indeed, the body does not consist of one member but of many. If the foot would say, "Because I am not a hand, I do not belong to the body," that would not make it any less a part of the body. And if the ear would say, "Because I am not an eye, I do not belong to the body," that would not make it any less a part of the body. If the whole body were an eye, where would the hearing be? If the whole body were hearing, where would the sense of smell be? But as it is, God arranged the members in the body, each one of them, as he chose. If all were a single member, where would the body be? As it is, there are many members, yet one body. The eye cannot say to the hand, "I have no need of you," nor again the head to the feet, "I have no need of you." On the contrary, the members of the body that seem to be weaker are indispensable, and those members of the body that we think less honorable we clothe with greater honor, and our less respectable members are treated with greater respect; whereas our more respectable members do not need this. But God has so arranged the body, giving the greater honor to the inferior member, that there may be no dissension within the body, but the members may have the same care for one another. If one member suffers, all suffer together with it; if one member is honored, all rejoice together with it. (1 Corinthians 12:12−26)

There is something about Paul's letter to the Corinthians that
rings true for us. At some level we have a sense that what affects
one of us affects all of us. Yet, we live in an era in which we find
it difficult to affect change beyond our immediate environment.
We feel powerless in relationship to governmental structures,
religious institutions and corporate conglomerates. At times we
feel like just another cog in the wheel that keeps an institution, a
corporation or a system going. However, Paul's Letter to the
Corinthians reminds us that our individual lives can and do
impact the whole.

This too is the message of Jesus' life. Jesus was one person. One
person who refused to go along with the tribe. One person who
interpreted the law in a new way. One person who refused to
accept the status quo. One person who challenged the way things
had always been done. We stand in the wake of one man who
walked the earth more than two thousand years ago.

Jesus walked this earth and lived his life in the way that he did
so that we might follow in his footsteps with wisdom gained from
his own transformation, his own journey through birth, death
and resurrection. His life is radical proof that our individual
transformation can have an enormous impact on the transformation of others. While this can sound somewhat idealistic, there
can be no doubt that we can and do affect one another—by the
thoughts we hold, the intentions that guide us and the by the
actions we take or refuse to take.

Surely each of us can recall a person or interaction that
changed the course of our lives. Maybe it was our spouse, a par-
ent, a teacher, a friend or a child. It may have even been a

stranger. Jesus' life is proof that what we do in our little corner of the world matters and may have an impact well beyond what we perceive the impact to be.

Paul's letter challenges us to see that there is a dynamic relationship between the parts and the whole. *What* we do with our lives and *why* we do it has ethical, philosophical and spiritual implications. Jesus' own life reveals that the choices we make and our reasons for making them can greatly impact the unfolding realities of our lives, and not just for ourselves.

Martin Luther King, Jr., in his Memphis speech addressing the sanitation workers' strike said it this way: "...either we go up together or we go down together. [So] let us develop a kind of dangerous unselfishness."[4] Jesus lived his life with the kind of dangerous unselfishness Martin Luther King, Jr., was calling for.

Redemption, freedom and liberation are not individual achievements. They can only be communal. Unless all of us are redeemed, unless all of us are free, none of us are. Until a critical mass employs the kind of dangerous unselfishness Martin Luther King, Jr., called for and Jesus actually lived, the kingdom will continue to elude us because we fail to recognize that we are on this journey together.

To become like God, dangerously unselfish, we have to become lavish sharers and people of opulent generosity. This means sharing what we have even when it hurts. This does not mean safely setting aside the leftovers or the extras. It means sharing what we have even if it is the last piece of bread we have. It does not mean forgoing the bread altogether. It means each person sharing the last piece of bread.

Developing this kind of dangerous unselfishness implies putting less energy into worshiping Jesus and more energy into becoming Jesus lest we diminish the impact that our own life can have in the transformation of the world, in the evolution of consciousness, and bringing about the kingdom of God right here and right now. Paul's First Letter to the Corinthians says in its final verses of chapter 12, "Now you are the body of Christ and individually members of it." Our lives matter. And what we do with them or what we fail to do with them impacts the whole.

As members of the body of Christ we have the power to breathe new life into a world that is crying out for healing and justice. We have the power to breathe new hope into situations wrought with despair. We have the power to breathe comfort into a world that is riddled with disease. Jesus' life reveals that an ordinary life given to prayer and good works can have an impact and radiance beyond the boundaries of the imaginable and can spark in others the fire of love and compassion, of generosity and selflessness, of peace and justice necessary for healing the world. These are the building blocks of the kingdom! We must make these our foundation if we are serious about following the footsteps of Jesus and attaining freedom.

Isn't this why we gather in community at all? Not just to imitate Jesus, but to become Jesus? Not just to pray for the coming of God's kingdom but to make it real in this time and this place? Let us take Martin Luther King's challenge "to develop a kind of dangerous unselfishness" in ourselves and in our communities. Let us do this together so we can meet the world, the church and one another with greater determination to be what we know we are—free and equal members in the Body of Christ.

P R A C T I C E

Ego Identification Exercise

Inertia, resisting change, failing to be proactive about our physical, emotional or spiritual health is the result of giving into our egos. In your journal make a list of the changes you know you need to make. For example, you may need to make improvements to your eating and exercise habits or give attention to your spiritual life or address a relationship in need of some work. Write down a few things you can do this week to begin to make the changes you know you need to make and do them!

Contemplation

Use the "not mine" exercise found on page 52. What does this exercise reveal to you about yourself?

Prayer

Generous and abundant God, stretch me into becoming dangerously unselfish. Let my family, friends, neighbors and even my enemies find you in me. Bountiful God in whose image I am made, give me opportunities to share the abundance you have given me. Teach me to rely on you for all my needs. Amen.

Action of Loving-kindness

This week anonymously do an act of loving-kindness for someone who goes largely unnoticed. For example, you could send flowers to someone who is going through a difficult time, or someone who is lonely or confined to their home. Or drop off a cup of hot coffee to the homeless person you pass on your way to work.

CHAPTER FOUR

PRACTICE! PRACTICE! PRACTICE!

The LORD is my light and my salvation;
   whom shall I fear?
The LORD is the stronghold of my life;
   of whom shall I be afraid?

When evildoers assail me
   to devour my flesh—
my adversaries and foes—
   they shall stumble and fall.

Though an army encamp against me,
   my heart shall not fear;
though war rise up against me,
   yet I will be confident. (Psalm 27:1–3)

Becoming a pilgrim on the path of transformation begins by actively discerning when we are feeding the good wolf and when we are feeding the evil wolf. We must choose how we will develop ourselves. Once the initial steps on the road to transformation are taken, there is no turning back. That is, once we acknowledge that we have the potential to empower the development of the Christ consciousness and the ability to restrict the influence of our ego, we can never go back to being blindly influenced by the ego. Once we awaken to our choice, we cannot assume the role of victim any longer as we trod the path of life.

The transformation journey will gift us and challenge us for a lifetime. There will be ups and downs, peaks and valleys. So ready yourself because this journey demands not only that we be radically and perpetually honest with ourselves and God, but it also demands that we make ourselves available to God by developing a steadfast practice of prayer and contemplation.

Through devotion to practice, we return again and again to the Word within and enter more deeply into the mystery of God. Practice is like weight-lifting for the soul. It strengthens our spiritual muscle and contributes to our ability to make choices from a position of trust, aligned with the Word within, rather than from a position of fear or defensiveness, which indicates the ego is involved.

The essence of developing a spiritual practice is developing awareness. Awareness! Awareness! Awareness! The ultimate goal of developing a consistent practice of prayer, contemplation and engaging in acts of loving-kindness is to perceive our interconnection with God, one another and all of life in every moment.

When we can come to rely on that perspective as our primary perspective, when we saturate ourselves in that awareness, we remain open and malleable because we trust that all things work together for the good of God. *All* things.

Spiritual practice also provides the training ground for discerning the difference between the drive and desires that stem from ego and the drive and desires that stem from the Word within. The impulse to grow into our potential, to live a meaningful life, to impact the world in a positive way is the Word within germinating in us. When we actually make life choices that positively impact ourselves and the world we live in, we develop new ways of being and perceiving that draw on and confirm the unity of all creation. By engaging in spiritual practices that reinforce our relationship with the Word within, our own divine nature grows stronger and eventually breaks through our lives as the Christ consciousness.

We call it a "practice" because that is precisely what it is. "Practice" implies repeated attempts in order to develop strength and skill. It also denotes an event that occurs with regularity. Any athlete desiring to overcome an opponent has to practice regularly. From day to day, the way the athlete practices may vary, but the goal of improving and strengthening one's skill remains. The same is true for a spiritual seeker. From day to day we may engage in various spiritual practices from contemplating a Scripture passage to practicing centering prayer to engaging in random or anonymous acts of loving-kindness. These various activities are practice drills whose aim is to increase and heighten our awareness of the sacredness of all life by realizing and acknowledging the Word within ourselves and all creation and committing to bringing that Word forth in our lives as the Christ consciousness in the world.

Though we have spoken primarily of prayer and contemplation as tools to connect with God and begin our transformation, we know too that if spirituality is about transformation, real transformation, it must manifest as action in the world. Prayer and contemplation are not enough. Action in the world is how we emulate and affirm Jesus' example in our lives. By his example, Jesus revealed that the act of feeding a hungry person is just as likely to bring us to transformation as prayer and contemplation. One practice does not outweigh another. The efficiency of any practice to transform us varies for each one of us.

As the psalmist states, this process of transformation, this journey of becoming requires that we be strong and take heart because it asks nothing less of us than everything. Still, if we are committed to pursuing this pilgrimage, the journey promises a life lived deeply rather than superficially. However, time is of the essence.

We cannot keep putting off our own transformation because nothing changes externally or in the world until you and I change internally. It does not serve our life's purpose to keep waiting for something better to come along. Andrew Cohen, a modern-day spiritual teacher and philosopher and author, warns about putting off this commitment to transformation. He says,

> Most of us are unwilling to be fully committed to life because we're waiting. The ego is always waiting for a better deal. But in a liberated relationship to life, we stop playing the waiting

game, because we realize this is it. This is everything, right now. And we recognize if we're not committed now, our relationship to life is inherently going to be superficial. The only reason so few of us live extraordinary lives is that we're not really committed. The minute we stop waiting for a better deal, and we are willing to be truly committed now, our lives become extraordinary. When we're that committed to this particular moment, which is every moment, we know that this is the best deal that there ever could be.[1]

We've got to dive into the life we've been given—with courage to face everything and avoid nothing, no matter how painful, no matter how diseased, no matter the intensity of feeling. But this kind of courage only comes from a deep conviction that we cannot be separated from God, and certain knowledge that we have been made in the image and likeness of God. We can only acquire this sense by drinking from the fountain of living water, by engaging in spiritual practices that refresh us and return our awareness to the ground of all being—the Word within. When we drink from that fountain, we nourish the natural inclination of the Word within to emerge through us as the Christ consciousness.

Expectations

> Let me sing for my beloved
>   my love-song concerning his vineyard:
> My beloved had a vineyard
>   on a very fertile hill.
> He dug it and cleared it of stones,
>   and planted it with choice vines;

he built a watch-tower in the midst of it,

and hewed out a wine vat in it;

he expected it to yield grapes,

but it yielded wild grapes. (Isaiah 5:1–2)

This passage from Isaiah reminds us that God has provided us with everything we need to bring forth a good harvest of justice and righteousness, which is another way of saying that God has given us everything we need to cultivate and bring forth the Christ consciousness. The playing field has been tilted in our favor. The vineyard has been prepared, and the necessary equipment provided to produce such an abundant harvest. Over and above that, God gave us guidelines by which to abide in order to preserve the fertility of the land and ensure an abundant crop of only good fruit.

God gave us everything we need to be free, whole, healthy and content. Everything we need to bring the kingdom about. Everything necessary to succeed, to grow into the people God hopes we will be. We are the choice vines planted in God's vineyard! And being "choice" means we have all the right stuff to succeed. We are preprogrammed for greatness. We have been specially picked to be planted here in this vineyard.

This is the vineyard—these cosmos, this planet, the nation, city, neighborhood, community and family in which we find ourselves. Too often we fail to see what we have right in front of us. We fail to see that we have everything we need. We take for granted the world in which we find ourselves and throw it to the wasteland every time we choose bitterness over joy, hatred over love, selfishness over selflessness.

We disregard the vineyard that has been prepared for us when we fail to see that all things, people and nature are interconnected. We strip the land of its bounty when we use the resources given us as a means to gaining personal or national wealth and distinction rather than working to attain mutuality and equality between genders, races and classes. In so doing, we pollute the environment that was once ready-made for our success, for producing abundance and bearing fruit. As a result, it is difficult for the Christ consciousness to blossom in us and flourish in the world.

When we choose prejudice rather than acceptance, when we choose to hold a grudge instead of letting go, or give the cold shoulder instead of a warm heart we find ourselves among the thorns and brambles. We denigrate the vineyard every time we choose to gossip or tear down by holding violent or hateful thoughts about others and even ourselves. We create obstructions to our own and other's natural impulse to evolve and transform when we stop believing in one another. We stunt our ability to grow when we begin to believe that we and others are incapable of change.

In fact, the reading from Isaiah continues to explain what happens when we pollute the vineyard God gave us: God wants no part of it. God lets the vineyard be trampled and does not prune or hoe. In other words, when we live embedded in the desires of ego, we live wanting only for ourselves. We squeeze God out altogether and forget that the power of love to affect and transform this world—so overcome with self-created pain and misery—is entirely dependent upon us! The power of love to affect and transform this world is entirely dependent upon us and the choices we make.

This is why we must become conscious and conscientious of our thoughts, intentions, and motivations. With every thought, word and deed we either choose to align ourselves with ego or we stand firmly in the ground of our being—the Word within. Only when we are firmly rooted in the Word within does the Christ consciousness have the opportunity to emerge through us and into the world.

When we live only to feed our ego, we produce an unfriendly environment, not conducive to growth and transformation. When we are rooted in the needs and wants of ego, we are self-consumed and preoccupied with our own pain, our own grief, our own accomplishments. We want only for ourselves and see ourselves as separate not only from one another, the earth and the entire cosmos, but most importantly, we see ourselves as separate from God. We feel that the hopes and dreams we have for our life are somehow separate from God's hopes and dreams for us.

When we align ourselves with the Word within, rather than identifying with ego, we realize that we are whole and one with God and all that is. As a result, we are more able to contribute positively to the "vineyard" given us which results in creating a fertile and supportive environment for soul development, which is necessary if we are going to fulfill our destiny and live up to our potential as children of God.

On the contrary, when we align ourselves with the desires of ego or champion our own selfish wants and desires, we actually become insecure and needy because we are constantly looking outside ourselves for the treasure that can only be found within.

And instead of cultivating a rich harvest, we cultivate thorns and brambles that leave us with a sense of isolation. Consequently, we begin to perceive ourselves as unworthy or impoverished and insufficient in some way. Thus, we never fully embrace the possibility that our lives really matter and we never strive to achieve the highest expression of our relationship with God, which is necessary for our own transformation and that of the world.

Remember, just because we were given the vineyard, ready-made for success, it does not mean we do not have to do any work. We still have to weed and water the crop. Weeding and watering are the work we have to do on ourselves.

Weeding, the work of restricting the growth and influence of ego, occurs when we work to rid ourselves of jealousy, bitterness, false pride and unkind thoughts we hold about others and ourselves. The need to weed calls us to be diligent in identifying those places in our hearts and minds that have become hardened, cynical or resigned to mediocrity. These are aspects of ego that threaten the vitality of the Word within. If the weeds or desires of ego grow out of control, they suppress the chances of the Word within growing to fullness and being unleashed in the world as the Christ consciousness.

As in any garden, the garden of our soul needs watering too. Prayer, contemplation and acts of loving-kindness water and nourish the Word within. Every time we step out of ourselves and reach out to another, we nourish this vineyard. Every time we express empathy and compassion and we are able to put ourselves in another's shoes, we feed our natural impulse to evolve into the person, people and community God seeded us to be.

God wants us to be untangled and untied from our ego so the Christ consciousness can grow unobstructed in us and be unleashed in the world. Jesus came into this vineyard to show us how to make the most of what we've been given. He reminded us that we have everything we need to bring forth this consciousness right here and right now. Make no mistake about it—we bear the responsibility for the condition of the vineyard and bringing forth its harvest.

Use It or Lose It

For it is as if a man, going on a journey, summoned his slaves and entrusted his property to them; to one he gave five talents, to another two, to another one, to each according to his ability. Then he went away. The one who had received the five talents went off at once and traded with them, and made five more talents. In the same way, the one who had the two talents made two more talents. But the one who had received the one talent went off and dug a hole in the ground and hid his master's money. After a long time the master of those slaves came and settled accounts with them. Then the one who had received the five talents came forward, bringing five more talents, saying, "Master, you handed over to me five talents; see, I have made five more talents." His master said to him, "Well done, good and trustworthy slave; you have been trustworthy in a few things, I will put you in charge of many things; enter into the joy of your master." And the one with the two talents also came forward, saying, "Master, you handed over to me two talents; see, I have made two more talents." His master said to him, "Well done, good and trustworthy slave; you have been trustworthy in a few things, I will put you in charge of many things; enter into the joy of your master." Then the one who had received the one talent also came forward, saying, "Master, I knew that you were a harsh man, reaping where you did not sow, and gathering where you did not scatter seed; so I was afraid, and I went and hid your talent in the ground. Here you have what is yours." But his master replied, "You wicked and lazy slave! You knew, did you, that I reap where I did not sow, and gather where I did not scatter? Then you ought to have invested my money with the bankers, and on my return I would have received what was my own with interest. So take the talent from him, and give it to the one with the ten talents. For to all those who have, more will be given, and they will have an abundance; but from those who have nothing, even what they have will be taken away." (Matthew 25:14–29)

Cultivating the Word within begins with belief—belief that we have been made in the image and likeness of God and therefore belief that within each one of us are "talents" waiting to be used, invested in and shared. In order to break open the parable of the talents, we have to consider the vantage point of the storyteller.

When we put ourselves in the place of Jesus, the storyteller, the parable breaks open. Of course the master was angered at the slave who buried the talent! Jesus is warning us—"Don't buy it! Don't believe for one minute that you have nothing to offer, nothing to contribute, nothing to bring to the world—no matter who says so, no matter who deems it, no matter how sacred the institution that declares it." With this parable Jesus is saying, "No matter how legitimate a case is made—do not believe for one minute that you have nothing to offer, nothing to contribute, nothing to bring to this world."

Think about it for a moment. Jesus is telling us that we can count on the fact that we have been made in God's image regardless of who would have us believe otherwise. In this parable Jesus assures us that we can rely on the truth that within each one of us is a treasure to be invested in, brought forth and shared. The treasure we each can count on is the Word within. By bringing it forth and sharing it with others it becomes the Christ consciousness.

In fact, go back to the parable and read again the response of the third slave to the master. The slave senses that the master expects something of him. Sensing that he has been entrusted with something very precious to the master and fearful that what he had been given could be foolishly spent, he buries the talent entrusted him in the ground. Clearly, the master has more faith in this slave than the slave does in himself. The one to whom the least was given does not trust his own capacity to produce abundance or make something good from what he has been given. He underestimates his capacity to contribute positively and live up to his potential because of the obstacles he perceives. This is a bold message for each one of us.

It is a reminder that the Word of God is contained in each of us, and every one of us is called to bring forth that Word, that divine potential, as the Christ consciousness, by manifesting in this life the gifts we have been given. When we trust that we have been made in the image and likeness of God, regardless of who or what may deem otherwise, the Christ consciousness has the possibility of emerging in and through us. Jesus' life reinforces this message.

Jesus identified with the women, lepers, tax collectors and prostitutes. He stood with the oppressed and disenfranchised. He identified with the outcasts and this caused some to question his own character and social standing. However, Jesus did not allow this to prohibit him from living the life he knew God was calling him to live. Jesus did not let others define him. He did not see himself as a helpless victim of the circumstances dealt him. He was defined solely by his relationship with God. With his life, Jesus says to each one of us, "Do not believe for one minute that you are not worthy of God's love. Do not believe that you are somehow tainted, unlovable, or empty of God's presence altogether. Do not believe that you are confined, disadvantaged or restricted in any way from fully investing yourself in this life regardless of the obstacles faced or challenges to overcome. No matter who says so. No matter how many others believe otherwise. No matter the real or perceived obstacles in your way. Rely on the truth that you have been "fearfully and wonderfully made" (Psalm 139:14).

This parable tells us that we can trust that our lives have value. We do not have to look for this to be confirmed by someone else, affirmed by society or ordained by any institution. God has confirmed it by bringing us into being. The heart of this parable's teaching calls us to take responsibility for the gifts we have been given and the life we have to bring them forth. It challenges us to freely invest and use our gifts as Jesus did—as a means to healing, reconciliation and communion, as well as to the cause of liberating others from the self-held belief that their lives hold little value or that life itself has no meaning.

When we find ourselves discounted, devalued or displaced, Jesus' life reminds us that our lives do indeed have meaning and that each one of us has to account for what we do with the gifts God has entrusted with us. Make no mistake about it, being made in God's image has demanding implications and what we do with what we have been given establishes the nature of our relationship with God and the nature of our relationships with each other.

PRACTICE

Ego Identification Exercise

Take some time to write in your journal and reflect on the ways you sabotage your own growth. Begin with writing down the relentless thoughts or self-talk you use to persuade yourself to believe you are not enough or you don't have what it takes to authentically engage in this life. It can be thoughts that sound like, "I'm such a loser," or, "I'm so stupid," or, "I'm so fat and ugly," or, "I've tried a hundred times to make a change. Obviously, I'm not strong enough to do it."

Write down anything that comes to your mind. Do not censor your writing. Be as honest with yourself as possible.

Identifying these thoughts allows us to protest them and replace them with affirmations. For example, any time we feel down on ourselves or disappointed in ourselves, instead of dwelling on the disappointment, we can initiate the mantra, "I am loved just as I am."

Contemplation

Consider your life as a vineyard. What shape is your vineyard in? Is it overtaken with weeds—self-consumption, narcissism and greed? What watering and weeding is needed to improve the conditions of your relationship with God?

Prayer

Giver of Life, awaken me to the gifts you have planted in me. I promise to use them responsibly and well in the service of faith, hope and love. May the gifts you've entrusted with me grow to fullness so that they may nourish those who hunger for a taste of you. Amen.

Action of Loving-kindness

Call a friend or drop a thank-you note to someone not expecting it. Use it as an opportunity to express gratitude for their friendship and the gifts with which this relationship blesses you.

CHAPTER FIVE

SETTING OUT

And the Spirit immediately drove him out into the wilderness.
He was in the wilderness forty days, tempted by Satan; and he
was with the wild beasts; and the angels waited on him. (Mark
1:12–13)

Being led or driven to the wilderness is nothing new for the spiritual pilgrim or the searcher. It is integral to pursuing the spiritual path, cultivating the Word within and calling the Christ consciousness forth. We have a long spiritual history that tells us time and time again of those who set out for the wilderness, the unknown. Any time we embrace the unknown by courageously going where we feel God is leading us, we are aligning ourselves with the Word within and allowing it to direct our lives rather than giving into our conditioning, which always prefers what is known, whether it works for good or not. When the drive and desires of ego are the primary motivating force in our lives, we end up clinging to the comfortable and expending all our energy in attempt to preserve the predictable.

So setting out—expanding our boundaries, starting anew, immersing ourselves from time to time in the unfamiliar—is a crucial component of evolution and transformation because it requires that we let go of someone or something, some way of being or relating in order to embrace the unknown and begin again. When life forces us to begin again, in a new place, with changed relationships, or from a different perspective, we are pressed to develop unproven skills and bring wisdom to maturity by letting go and beginning again. Indeed, setting out is a recurring requirement for any pilgrim on the path of transformation. Even Jesus was forced to set out for the wilderness of the unknown. In so doing, he followed the footsteps of his spiritual ancestors.

The Hebrew Scriptures tell us that Abraham and Sarah were simply instructed to leave. In Genesis, God said to them: "Go from your country and your kindred and your father's house to the land that I will show you" (12:1). They were not given a map. They had no idea where they were going. There was no clear destination on the horizon. They were simply told to leave what they knew for the unknown. In response to God's urging, Abraham and Sarah stepped through the threshold of the familiar into the wilderness of the unknown.

This is the setting out required by every spiritual pilgrim at least once, but more likely several times in a lifetime. Sometimes the setting out requires that we leave behind the things, people, and environment that we love the most or that provides the most comfort and stability in our lives. For Abraham and Sarah it meant not only leaving their relatives and loved ones, but their setting out required that they leave behind the geography they had come to build their lives around and the social network that had supported them. They also had to let go of any preconceptions or assumptions about how their lives would unfold from that point forward.

Once they set out they could no longer expect relationships, language or culture to be familiar. They could not rely on past experience to inform their future because the territory they would be covering was foreign to them in every way. They did not know where they were going or how long they would be on the journey. They could only rely on the Word of God to lead them to their destiny.

Setting out, the Torah reveals, is an integral part of the spiritual journey. Not only were Abraham and Sarah told to set out, but in the next generation Isaac had to set out with his father. Genesis

22:2 states, "Take your son, you only son, Isaac, whom you love...". As Abraham had to leave his father, Isaac had to leave his mother. And then in the next generation, Jacob had to set out, leaving behind his father, and his mother and his brother. Genesis 28:10 says, "Jacob left Beersheba...". And then in the next generation, Joseph had to set out, leaving behind brothers, mother and father. Genesis 37:28 states, "And they took Joseph to Egypt...". And then the Torah records that Moses, too, had to set out. Exodus 2:15 states, "Moses fled," leaving behind his people. Again, another one moved by the word of God to set out for the wilderness of the unknown.

Finally in Exodus 13 we hear that, "God led the people by the roundabout...way of the wilderness." God brought an *entire people*, a whole community, out into the wilderness where they could encounter both the immanence and transcendence of God.

The Gospels tell us that Jesus, too, was driven to the wilderness of preparation, so that he might set out on his way to fulfilling his destiny as the Christ. The Scriptures say, "Then Jesus was led up by the Spirit into the wilderness" (Matthew 4:1). Jesus' journey into the wilderness, where he was tempted by Satan, marks the beginning of his public ministry. Indeed this was the beginning of an entirely new life for him.

Most of us find ourselves in the wilderness, not because we willingly accept an invitation, but because we have been driven there. We may find ourselves in the wilderness because something in our life has changed so drastically that we do not know who we are anymore. Our relationship to life itself changes.

In the wilderness many of the things that comforted us or gave us a feeling of security make us feel empty now. We no longer find pleasure in the things that once gave us pleasure. We no longer find satisfaction in the things that once fulfilled us. We no longer find meaning in the relationships or rituals in which we have engaged for years. Devastating loss or momentous change in a primary relationship can land us in the wilderness when we least expect it. Most of us don't enter the wilderness willingly, we find ourselves there reluctantly.

Just think about the groaning and complaining of the Israelites. Moses promised them freedom. Freedom! And God promised them more abundance than they could imagine—a land flowing with milk and honey! But while they were enduring the wilderness, they longed to return to Egypt, to Pharaoh. They were desperate to return to slavery, to a life lived according to someone else's desires. They were willing to put their lives back in the hands of slave drivers rather than endure the wilderness, simply because it was known. It was familiar. It was predictable.

Regardless of how we get there, setting out, encountering the wilderness is a necessary part of the spiritual path and integral to life itself. Like turning over the soil to prepare for the new planting season, the wilderness prepares us for an entirely new way of being. The wilderness represents the end of one life and the beginning of a completely new relationship to life itself.

Most of us will find ourselves entering the wilderness again and again throughout our lives because it is a necessary part of cultivating a relationship with the Word within and bringing forth greater and more powerful expressions of the Christ consciousness in the world. In the wilderness we have a tendency to return to dependency on God, to call out and urgently seek God's guidance. The stark simplicity of the wilderness strips us of comfort and forces us to experience life from a new perspective. It does not allow us to engage in life as usual.

One after another, our spiritual ancestors, with their deep desire for freedom and yearning for something more, responded to the Word of God, which called them out of slavery, out of one way of being into the river of transformation. Often these spiritual pilgrims were led away from not only their physical surroundings and familial relationships, but they also had to let go of their expectations, their narrow way of seeing things and the predictability they had come to rely upon.

The spiritual path requires that we, like our ancestors, set out from time to time. Through change, loss and challenge we are forced to leave our preconceptions, habits and obligations for the wilderness of no expectations, but unimaginable possibilities. We can be sure that we too will be called by God to set out at least once and probably many times throughout our lives. Maybe it's because we search so desperately for God when we travel into the unknown. Maybe it's because we rely on God more readily in the wilderness. Whatever the reason, the paths trod by our spiritual ancestors remind us that setting out is not just required at the beginning of the spiritual journey. It is a significant and standard part of what it means to be a pilgrim on the path of transformation.

The wilderness is not just a desert through which our ancestors in faith wandered for forty years. It isn't just a place that Jesus lingered for forty days and forty nights. It is a way of being. It is an experience that demands our attention and requires profound openness to the flow of life around us. It is an experience that demands being fully present to God, to the unknown. In the wilderness possessions do not comfort us. Preconceptions cannot protect us. Logic alone cannot map out our future. In the wilderness we are left alone each day with an experience of God that astonishes, refines and reveals.

In the wilderness we learn that God is with us—always. Yes, God is there—when one thing ends and another begins, in the spaces in between. As we make our way through the wildernesses of our lives, we are awakened to realize that we have been destined to set out all along because transformation is the purpose of our lives and real transformation, transformation at the root of the soul, occurs when we allow the Word of God to guide us to our destiny even if it means encountering the wilderness or going through the desert to get there.

Our spiritual ancestors set out for and traversed the wilderness many times. It was integral to their becoming the people God was calling them to be. Setting out for and enduring the wilderness is part of every spiritual journey because it requires that we let go and begin again, let go and begin again, let go and begin again. Demanding in its simplicity and insisting on change and letting go, the wilderness promises a new way of being.

Letting Go

> When he had come near Bethphage and Bethany, at the place called the Mount of Olives, he sent two of the disciples, saying, "Go into the village ahead of you, and as you enter it you will find tied there a colt that has never been ridden. Untie it and bring it here. If anyone asks you, 'Why are you untying it?' just

say this, 'The Lord needs it.' " So those who were sent departed and found it as he had told them. As they were untying the colt, its owners asked them, "Why are you untying the colt?" They said, "The Lord needs it." Then they brought it to Jesus; and after throwing their cloaks on the colt, they set Jesus on it. As he rode along, people kept spreading their cloaks on the road. As he was now approaching the path down from the Mount of Olives, the whole multitude of the disciples began to praise God joyfully with a loud voice for all the deeds of power that they had seen, saying,

> "Blessed is the king
>> who comes in the name of the Lord!
> Peace in heaven,
>> and glory in the highest heaven!" (Luke 19:29–38)

Just as the Israelite's journey from slavery to freedom is a metaphor for our own spiritual journey, Jesus' journey from Galilee to Jerusalem is also a path of transformation promising liberation for all of us should we take it up ourselves. This journey, like that of the Israelites', if it is to transform us, demands radical openness. To be open is about allowing ourselves to be vulnerable, to be exposed from the inside out. That is, we have to be willing to let go of pretense, let go of thinking that we have all the answers, let go of excuses, let go of prejudice and judgment and give ourselves to the process of birth, death and resurrection with as much honesty, integrity and transparency as Jesus did.

Luke's Gospel tells us that those who gathered to welcome Jesus removed their cloaks and laid them on the ground as Jesus made his final entry into Jerusalem. If we desire to welcome the Word into our hearts and make ourselves a dwelling place for the

Lord, we too must remove our cloaks. The cloaks we wear are not made of fabric. Rather, the cloaks we wear serve as the protective covering over our hearts. Disappointing relationships, personal failures and broken trust can, if we allow them, become the cloaks to which we cling, preventing access to our hearts. We can also cling to poor self-images, opinionated assumptions and confining prejudices in order to protect ourselves and keep others, even God, at bay. In laying down our "cloaks," we allow ourselves to be exposed to those things that weather us, shape us and challenge us to grow in ways we may never have thought possible.

If Jesus' life is to have any real chance of leading us to transformation, we have to acknowledge those experiences and relationships that have hardened our hearts or calloused us in some way. We have to be willing to face honestly the ways that we close ourselves off or reject the transforming power of God's Word to inspire us to change.

Laying down our cloaks begins by consciously discerning how our attitudes and beliefs either open us to greater possibilities and potential or close us off from experiencing ourselves, our relationships and the world in new ways. Life's landscape is littered with births, deaths and resurrections, and all of these experiences involve some degree of letting go. Of these, it is the deaths we encounter along the journey that usually sear us with pain or demand more from us than we even believe we are capable of realizing. The letting go that death demands can be excruciating. Yet, the path of Jesus insists that death too is a cloak disguising another entrance to God and an opportunity for profound transformation.

Death comes in many forms—in losses, big and small, in leaving a job or vocation, in leaving a relationship, the death of a loved one or the decline of our own bodies. Death is any process of letting go, of walking farther into the wilderness not knowing where the path may lead or what outcome may result. Letting go is difficult, to be sure, but it is the only way we keep our hearts warm and moist, retaining a malleable quality that leaves us open to change and restores our forgiving nature.

Holding on to that which is ripe for letting go sours the soul and denies the regenerative power of God. Clinging to that which is no longer life-giving is a choice to remain closed. It is a choice for self-protection and hardness of heart. It is a choice for cleaving to the cloak, withholding and resisting the letting go necessary for ushering in new life. It is a choice for stagnation rather than stretching. And this is the path to prison, not liberation.

Trusting that God is with us through it all and courageously expecting God to bring new life out of even the crudest circumstances, hope from the most devastating losses and wisdom from life's blows that strike us dumb is how we place ourselves in the footprints of Jesus. Embracing death as a portal to new life is how we remove the cloak that covers our heart and stymies our growth.

When we trust that God's presence is at every juncture of our life's journey, as Jesus did, we are better able to make choices for opening rather than closing, choices for awareness rather than avoidance, choices for dialogue rather than denial, choices for compassion rather than judgment and choices for growth rather than comfort. Jesus' life affirms that when we live from this kind of foundation of trust in God, we begin to leave in our wake a path to resurrection and rebirth. We begin to leave in our wake a different reality, a new way of being and relating to others. We begin to leave in our wake pathways to transformation and footprints to freedom.

Jesus' own entry into Jerusalem challenges us to enter our own experiences of death, loss and change with confidence that God is there. Trusting God in such conditions demands that we remain open to new life and resist our inclination to judge or draw sweeping conclusions about the nature of our experience or the nature of life itself until the letting go is complete and we can see new life in what was previously uninhabitable. In order for this to occur, we have to resist the temptation to withhold or protect our hearts when what is needed most is openness, acceptance, forgiveness and compassion.

No one said this would be an easy journey. Trusting that God is with us and available to us every moment on this journey demands courage, strength and extraordinary willingness to love and forgive ourselves and others, again and again and again. Learning to let go—even in the midst of trial and trepidation—is vital to the process of becoming, mending our hearts and healing our world!

Just when we want to close off, protect ourselves, withdraw or hide out, just when we want to lash out in defense, Jesus' life challenges us to be open and exposed. We see an example of this in Luke's Gospel (22:1) when Jesus is approached in the garden of Gethsemane by one of the guards who come to arrest him. As Jesus and his friends are confronted in the garden, one of his followers becomes defensive and retaliates in anger, cutting off the ear of a high priest's servant. Instead of letting this act of violence escalate, Jesus reaches out and heals the one who had come to arrest and detain him.

Many of us may have responded like Jesus' follower, reacting in a defensive, resistant and angry way, but Jesus, standing firm in what he knew to be true, responds to violence and hatred with nonviolence, even offering healing. This is openness! This is freedom! This kind of restraint and ability to choose nonviolence in the midst of a violent and threatening circumstance on the part of Jesus, and on our part when we are able to invoke it, creates a possibility for transformation not only on the part of the victim of violence, but also in the heart of the perpetrator of the violent act.

Another example of the transforming power of openness and vulnerability is expressed in the Stations of the Cross with the story of Jesus' meeting with Veronica. Exhausted and anguished, Jesus makes his way through the streets of Jerusalem when Veronica, a woman in the crowd moved with compassion, wipes his face and cares for him.

By this time on the journey, most of us would have lost all faith in humanity, and at the very least, flinched when we saw another hand coming at our face. But Jesus, precisely at the moment when he could have justifiably doubted love's possibility to endure, rests his worn face in Veronica's hands and lets her love him. What trust!

Again and again Jesus shows us that letting go is imperative to the process of transformation and living to our potential. While hanging on the cross, Jesus continues to show us how to let go when he says to the one hanging next to him, "Today you will be with me in the kingdom." And again when he says, with all he has left, "Father, into your hands I commend my spirit." With his last words, Jesus lets go of the life he knew for an entirely new kind of life altogether.

Jesus' journey reminds us again and again that letting go is fundamental to our ability to be transformed. Our capacity to change and be changed is directly proportional to our ability to let go, to forgive and be forgiven. Committing ourselves to this kind of radical openness, especially when we are facing difficult or painful circumstances, creates the greatest possibility for transformation to occur and new life to emerge.

It takes great strength to let go when faced with loss or death of any kind. Developing this kind of strength is crucial to our ability to choose openness when everything in us wants to grab on and cling more tightly to the life we know. The freedom to choose to let go and the strength to actually do it is just what Jesus modeled for us.

We will know when we have chosen the transformative path of Jesus when we are faced with the opportunity to harden, to close, to protect ourselves—but instead choose to soften, to open further, to give ourselves again. We can be sure we are following in the footsteps of Jesus when we choose to love even though we may be let down again, even though we may experience great pain again.

Letting go challenges us to recognize and grapple with the temporary nature of life. Eventually everything and everyone dies. We will inevitably be faced with letting go of those people and things we love the most, but choosing to give and receive love anyway is an act of extraordinary courage and a demonstration of remarkable trust in God and the process of transformation itself. Removing the cloaks that lay over our hearts promises to reveal the hidden passageway from death to new life, insisting then that resurrection is only available to those who are willing to let go in order to be transformed.

Jesus' journey from Galilee to Jerusalem is a wake-up call to every pilgrim on the spiritual path to stop living as if we have an infinite amount of time to change. The time is now! There is no time to withhold. There is no time to keep holding that grudge. There's no time to grow hard and bitter! We have got to live courageously and love well now! We have got to pursue healing and forgiveness today. Embracing change and transformation is how we fuel our own transformation and impel the Christ consciousness into action.

All the way to the end, Jesus freely chooses to let go again and again by remaining open, completely open, regardless of the fear, pain or rejection he endured. His life challenges us to do the same. Freely choosing love in the face of hatred, nonviolence in the face of violence, hope in the face of doubt and trust in the face of fear is the only way the Christ consciousness will become the consciousness of humanity. Until we claim the Christ consciousness as our own, peace will elude us, discomfort will consume us and violence will continue to come between us.

LOST AND FOUND

The LORD said to Moses, "Go down at once! Your people, whom you brought up out of the land of Egypt, have acted perversely; they have been quick to turn aside from the way that I commanded them." (Exodus 32:7-8)

The path of transformation is inherently challenging. It involves ups and downs, hills and valleys. There are times when we feel on top of the world and times when we feel the whole world has come crashing down upon us. The journey can be difficult and we can easily lose our footing and find ourselves lost. This can make it seem impossible to bear the unknown and leave us feeling desperate for some guidance or direction. Let us look back at the story of the Israelites' quest for freedom to see how they moved into the unknown, confronted the anxieties that come from feeling lost or disconnected from God.

Here's the deal: Moses had been gone for quite a while and the Israelites became really anxious, feeling that maybe even Moses abandoned them. Moses was the Israelites' "connection" to God. He was their "in" to the Promised Land. So here are the Israelites, out in the middle of nowhere, and Moses leaves them to go to the mountaintop to be alone with God. When Moses does not come back at the expected time, the Israelites give into their anxiety and begin to grasp at straws.

In Moses' absence the Israelites feel as if God has abandoned them. So in an effort to comfort the people, Aaron, with the help of others, creates a statue of a calf and says to the Israelites, "There! This is your God who brought you out of the land of Egypt." But that offends the one true God! In frustration, God says to Moses, in effect, "*Your* people! They can't feel me or sense me without your presence so what do they do? They try to comfort themselves without turning to me! They try to fill the hole of their doubt and despair with this nonliving, inanimate object! I'm going to wipe them all out and start over!"

Now we might not fashion a statue of a calf to ease our discomfort and improve our sense of security, but we might drink too much or work too much. We might bury our head in the sand in an effort not to feel the intensity of the reality we are facing. Whatever the "molten calf," we have to recognize that it does not serve in leading us to freedom or moving us toward our destiny. At some point we will realize that the molten calf is never a satisfying substitute for the real thing.

Moses pleads to God on behalf of the Israelites, reminding God that they are *God's* people! God's chosen! These are the ones to whom God has promised liberation and new life. And with Moses' pleading, God relents.

We all feel like Israelites sometimes. We feel that our lives are void of God or God's presence. We feel that something is missing or that something is wrong. We feel anxious about our future, about the direction our life is taking. There are times in life when we feel as if we are lost and other periods when we feel found.

Life, it seems, is really about enduring the cycles of being lost and found. As we trod the spiritual path of transformation, we are constantly moving between Jesus' cry from the cross, "My God, my God why have you forsaken me!" and Thomas's surprise when he realized Jesus was in his presence as the risen Christ— "My Lord and My God! It is you."

We all experience times when we feel lost. Our lives may feel directionless and we are certain that God has really abandoned us this time. Hope seems like a mirage and joy seems like a thing of

SETTING OUT | 93

the past. We may feel drained and empty of passion. We feel list-less. And the light at the end of the tunnel is a dim glimmer at best.

Yet there are times when each one of us feels "found" or part of the fold. We feel connected, cared for and supported. When we feel "found," we have a sense of God's presence with us. We feel certain that the Word within is alive in us. We feel that our lives have purpose, that God has a plan for us. We feel securely held. We may even have a sense of God's light surrounding us and hemming us in.

We can experience both extremes for various lengths of time. We may feel lost only for a day or two. Or it may be two or three, five, ten or even twenty years that we feel abandoned, alone in our suffering and disconnected from God. The same can be said for the experience of feeling found. It, too, can be a day, a month, a year or years.

In those times when God's presence cannot be felt, we may begin to entertain the idea that God may not exist at all. It can feel as if life is random and chaotic and holds no real meaning. Saint John of the Cross referred to this experience as the "dark night of the soul." Other mystics and sages of varying traditions have referred to the feeling of being lost as a "desert experience."

During such times, it is a good idea to find a spiritual compan-ion, a qualified spiritual director or licensed therapist who can walk the difficult journey with us, even if it is only to remind us that we do not traverse the journey of transformation alone. We are all pilgrims on this journey. When we are really feeling lost in life and we are unable to call out or communicate with God, when we are just sure the light in our lives has been extinguished for good this time, a spiritual director or spiritual companion—those with whom we can share our spiritual journey—can remind us that we are never alone.

Those who are willing to walk with us through the dark valleys of life become Moses for us. Like Moses, the one who travels with us into the desert or the wilderness pleads to God on our behalf during those times when we are unable to call out or communicate with God ourselves. Having someone in our lives who can do this for us is important because when we, like the Israelites, put our faith in the wrong things, when we fashion a molten calf out of our addictions or a desperate need for approval, for example, and cling to that rather than trusting God, a spiritual director or companion calls us back to trust in God. Like Moses, they can shake us loose from our infatuation with the idol and steer us back into the gaze of God.

Calling one another back to God, back to trust in the process of life, which relentlessly moves through birth, death and resurrection, is how we become Moses for one another. The communal nature of the journey to freedom and redemption challenges us to become one another's "connection" to God when we find ourselves or another lost or alone and unable to trust in God's presence. A spiritual companion or director communicates with God for us by giving voice to the prayers we cannot speak, securely holding the feelings that flood us, and easing the burden of despair we are certain we cannot bear alone.

When we feel lost we have to do whatever we can to get next to someone who is found, someone grounded in the Word within, certain of God's presence. We have to do whatever we can to get into the company of supportive people—or a supportive community—where we can be Moses for one another. You and I are one another's "connection" or "in" to God during those times when we have lost contact with our spiritual compass—the Word within.

Keeping a practice of prayer and contemplation, especially when we feel lost, is important because it gives God a chance to find us, a chance to reach us. It is in times like these that God becomes the woman looking for the lost coin and the shepherd searching for the lost sheep. Even if we can only pray or meditate for ten minutes a day, it reveals a deep trust that we will be found. It demonstrates a willingness to believe that even the experience of being lost is part of the transformation process. Even if we are only able to still our body from movement, but our mind remains restless during our prayer and contemplation time, it remains a signal to God that we desire to be found.

Coming to prayer and contemplation in times when we feel lost asks everything of us because we are saying with our body, mind and spirit that we still trust (or at least are trying to trust) when everything else in our lives feels questionable. Cultivating deep trust in God's ability to bring life from death, hope from despair and light from darkness is the essence of the spiritual journey. It is Jesus in the Garden asking God to find another way, but still giving everything of himself to trust that God could make good out of the circumstances that looked and actually were very bleak, very painful, and ultimately very costly.

Bringing ourselves to God through a consistent practice of prayer and contemplation, even or especially when we don't feel like it, is crucial to taking responsibility for our part in our relationship with God. It is not about coming to prayer and contemplation and expecting the heavens to open and God's voice to come booming out of the clouds. Maintaining a steadfast practice of prayer and contemplation is our way of signaling to God that we want what God wants for us more than anything else.

We are all on the path of transformation. All of us. It is a communal journey and that means that unless we traverse it together, unless all of us are free, none of us are free. So like Moses for the Israelites, we have to be willing to plead to God on behalf of one another. We have to be willing to be a connection or an "in" to God for those who can find no other way. We have to be willing to seek companionship or guidance from a qualified spiritual director when we feel lost, abandoned or confused about where the journey of transformation is taking us and what it is asking of us. This kind of relationship can facilitate our discernment about the direction God is calling us by helping us pay attention to the unfolding in our midst.

PRACTICE

Ego Identification Exercise

Spend some time journaling about one or two major changes in your life. It could be a change you entered into willingly, like a career change. Or it could be a change that came from life circumstances beyond your control. For example, the death of a friend or end of a significant relationship, a necessary move or change in lifestyle due to illness or the need to improve one's health.

Consider your emotional and spiritual state at the time of the change. Were you like the Israelites, grumbling about the difficulty or strain the change required of you? Or, were you able to remain open, aligned with the Word within, certain of God's presence with you during the change or shift in life circumstance?

Recall in your writing what your attitude was at the beginning of the change and how your attitude evolved as a result of the passage of time. Were you able to trust that God was with you throughout? Or, now that you are able to look back, what evidence do you see that God was with you?

Contemplation

Meister Eckhart once said, "There where clinging to things ends is where God begins to be."[1] What in your life is ripe for letting go? What do you need to enable this letting go?

Prayer

Jesus, you often comforted your disciples by saying, "Do not be afraid." Help me to trust, even when I feel lost, that you are with me. Give me courage to ask for help when I need it, especially when I feel lost and forsaken. Amen.

Action of Loving-kindness

This week be Moses for someone in need. Plead and pray to God on behalf of someone who is going through a difficult time. Keep this act of loving-kindness to yourself so as not to garner attention or praise from others.

CHAPTER SIX

PAY ATTENTION!

Wisdom is radiant and unfading,

and she is easily discerned by those who love her,

and is found by those who seek her.

She hastens to make herself known to those who desire her.

One who rises early to seek her will have no difficulty,

for she will be found sitting at the gate.

To fix one's thought on her is perfect understanding,

and one who is vigilant on her account will soon be free

   from care,

because she goes about seeking those worthy of her,

and she graciously appears to them in their paths,

and meets them in every thought. (Wisdom 6:12–16)

The mystical traditions agree that the universe we live in is revelatory, or as Jewish mystics say, encoded. They contend that there is a spark of the divine in all creation—not just in matter and material things, but in our thoughts, emotions, relationships and every life circumstance in which we find ourselves. The mystics from various traditions try to articulate in a myriad of ways that there is more to life than what meets the eye. Nothing is as it seems. Science tells us that the nature of life itself is that it unfolds and evolves. Within that unfolding, God meets us, calls forth our potential and surprises us.

Wisdom is constantly being revealed to us, not just through the spectacular, but even through the ordinary relationships and mundane activities of our lives. However, if we are not paying attention, if we are not anticipating Wisdom's presence, we will not perceive her presence. The reading tells us clearly that if we want to find Wisdom, we must seek her, look for her and expect her to be there. This passage implores us to pay attention.

Cultivating the ability to pay attention involves being able to own or acknowledge our prejudices and cultural biases, and philosophical leanings so that we can deliberately and consciously begin to examine, challenge, and possibly even change them. When we begin to identify those people, personalities or circumstances that snag us or provoke a strong reaction in us, we are engaging in the path of transformation because we are discerning the difference between those things that feed our ego and those things that feed our soul, which in turn fortifies our ability to bring forth the Christ consciousness through our lives.

In order to honestly discern our prejudices and biases we have to develop the capacity to observe ourselves. We have to cultivate within ourselves the ability to watch ourselves, our reactions, thoughts, feelings and emotions—without judgment. And that's the hard part. Yet it is the key to our own transformation.

By cultivating the observer in ourselves and paying attention, we begin to learn, see and understand just how and where we are not yet free. For example, when we react passionately about something, while passion can be a good thing, sometimes we are off and running with our feelings before really knowing where the conversation is going or before collecting all the facts that can inform our reaction. This can lead to important mistakes, hurtful exchanges and misleading assumptions.

Developing the capacity to observe ourselves without judgment is critical to our spiritual development. By observing ourselves without judgment, we become familiar with our "trouble spots" and are more empowered to choose to react or respond to those people, circumstances or feelings in a different way than we had before. It allows us to be more deliberate about the choices we make—whether it is choosing to use different words, a different tone or choosing to pursue a different course of action altogether. Exercising our ability to choose another way of being or relating invites the possibility of expressing the Christ consciousness more clearly through our choices, relationships and ultimately our lives.

Increasing our ability to pay attention begins with anticipating God's presence in all things. This is what it means to pay attention or stay awake. Jesus and other spiritual teachers and mystics from a variety of religious traditions often urged their followers to stay awake. Rumi chanted, "The breeze at dawn has secrets to tell you. Don't go back to sleep. You must ask for what you really want. Don't go back to sleep."[1] Developing the ability to pay attention is a commitment to look ceaselessly for Wisdom in all things. It reveals trust that sparks of the divine reside in all things—pleasure and pain, joy and sorrow, life and death. Wisdom will, however, remain concealed in our experiences and relationships unless we follow three rules.

Oftentimes children are taught to stop, look and listen before crossing the street. By adhering to these commands, accidents are prevented and fatal mistakes thwarted. Even today they help us pay attention to what is happening around us. These same three rules can also be applied to our spiritual lives and can be very instrumental in developing our ability to pay attention and observe ourselves and others without overreacting or dismissing the experience we are having.

Just think for a minute about what would have happened at the burning bush if Moses had not been paying attention. What if he had reacted to a feeling of fear and run in the other direction or tried to extinguish the fire without first observing it? He would have missed an encounter with God that ultimately called forth his potential and set him in the direction of his destiny.

By paying attention, Moses was able to observe the burning bush and hear the voice of God in it. Why? Because Moses employed the three rules critical to paying attention. He stopped, looked and listened.

> Moses said, "I must turn aside and look at this great sight, and
> see why the bush is not burned up." When the LORD saw that
> he had turned aside to see, God called to him out of the bush.
> "Moses, Moses!" And he said, "Here I am." Then [God] said,
> "Come no closer! Remove the sandals from your feet, for the
> place on which you are standing is holy ground." (Exodus
> 3:3–5)

Moses was standing in the place of an observer. The ability to pay
attention and stand in the place of an observer in relationship to
our experience is the holy ground we are called to stand upon if
we are serious about pursuing transformation. The ability to stop,
look and listen before reacting is the holy ground we must seek in
all our interactions if we truly desire to seek Wisdom, encounter
God and be changed by the experience.

Seeking this Holy Ground demands commitment to persevere,
to try again and again to develop the observer in ourselves—even
after we have exploded or overreacted or avoided something to
the point of neglect. It is never too late to develop the observer in
ourselves. That's the good news!

Humility is the primary virtue required for paying attention
because it suggests that we cannot presume to know what is happening. We have to leave open the possibility that something else
is going on, that there is more to the story than meets the eye. We
have to leave open the possibility that our immediate assessment
of the situation we are experiencing may only be partial and further insight may be gained upon later reflection.

Paying attention is not just about being alert. It implies the
ability to be still, to not move from that which is most important.

Moses was able to encounter God because he did not move from the holy ground of observation. He remained still in mind, body and spirit and as a result was able to hear the voice of God directly addressing him.

That same commitment to "not move" is truly the most difficult aspect of paying attention. It means not moving from the position of observer. Not moving from the unfolding. Not moving from a fundamental position of trust in God's presence, no matter the feeling, emotion or physical reality confronting us.

This is the essence of paying attention. This is what is demanded of each of us if we truly desire freedom. So the next time you feel an emotion overtaking you, or a situation in your life overwhelming you, let it be an indication to assume the position of Moses at the burning bush. Plant yourself firmly on that holy ground of observation so you can pay attention and not be consumed by the experience. Stop, look and listen and maybe you too will have an unimaginable encounter with God!

B E L I E V E !

As Jesus went on from there, two blind men followed him, crying loudly, "Have mercy on us, Son of David!" When he entered the house, the blind men came to him; and Jesus said to them, "Do you believe that I am able to do this?" They said to him, "Yes, Lord." Then he touched their eyes and said, "According to your faith let it be done to you." And their eyes were opened. Then Jesus sternly ordered them, "See that no one knows of this." But they went away and spread the news about him throughout that district. (Matthew 9:27–31)

Let's face it: Change is difficult for most of us. There are times when we feel that our way is the right way, certainly the best way, maybe even the only way. This kind of thinking reveals our own blind spots and exposes our closed-mindedness.

If we always think we have *the* way or *the* answer, we reveal our own arrogance and narcissism, leaving little room in our hearts for something new to surprise us and little chance of experiencing newness in ourselves or others. However, when we are able to leave our minds open for another possibility, even just a little bit, we find that even the smallest opening can lead to new insight and understanding.

The path of transformation constantly challenges us not only to be open but also to be profoundly receptive to the possibility of another way or an alternate reality. Jesus said to those whose eyes were opened in Matthew's Gospel, "According to your faith let it be done to you." He is saying that what we believe impacts our healing as well as that of the world. What we believe about ourselves, others and even God impacts our ability to be transformed!

Being committed to ongoing transformation implies that we always face an unknown future. It means never presuming to know where the journey might take us. Often, as we face the unknown, our own "blindness" readily surfaces in the form of fear, suspicion, negativity and possibly even hopelessness. But the good news is the blind men in this story held within themselves the necessary ingredient for their own healing, their own transformation—belief. Belief that they could change and be changed. Belief that they could gain a new perspective. Belief that life could be lived from an entirely different vantage point. Belief that life as they knew it could be radically altered and they would be OK—maybe even better than before.

As we embark on the path of transformation, we must be willing to ask ourselves again and again, "What attitudes and beliefs do I hold that keep me blind to the possibilities?" and "Can I, like the blind men in Matthew's Gospel, receive new information, take in fresh ideas, and live through different life experiences to the point of letting myself be changed by them?"

Transformation is the purpose of our lives. We follow the path of Jesus so we, like he, can be transformed by the births, deaths and resurrections that living entails. Change is the only way to grow into our potential. In fact, if we are the same person we were even one year ago, or five years ago, ten years ago or, God forbid, twenty years ago, if we haven't changed our mind, or our opinions, if we have not evolved spiritually, we aren't really living—not an engaged life anyway. Because absolutely everything in our lives is there for one reason and one reason alone: to offer us the opportunity to transform, to change our hearts, our minds and the way we relate to one another, God and all creation. Engaging in our own transformation is the way we can affect positive change in our lives and relationships, as well as in this world.

When we awaken to this perspective—that the work of our lives is transforming—we realize that no matter how far we have come, we all have to *continue* to change. There is no end to the process of transformation because it means never resisting growth and change at the deepest levels of our being. Such openness requires profound receptivity on our part because we can only change the world if we change ourselves, if we change our own selfish

desires, if we can—more often than not—take the position of realizing we do not know everything, we do not have all the answers
and we cannot guarantee what the future holds. In this way, we
begin to diligently rid ourselves of the tyrant, judge and know-it-
all that lives inside of us.

So as we move more deliberately into the path of transformation, let us become aware of the ways we resist change, limit our
own evolution and put a lid on our capacity for growth. Let us
look to one another and to our future inviting God to surprise us,
certain that we will be given plenty of opportunities to change
and be changed. In this way we prepare ourselves for possibilities
we cannot yet see and signal to God that we are ready for the
future God has planned for us.

POWER AND AUTHORITY

> They went to Capernaum; and when the Sabbath came, he
> entered the synagogue and taught. They were astounded at his
> teaching, for he taught them as one having authority, and not
> as the scribes. Just then there was in their synagogue a man
> with an unclean spirit, and he cried out, "What have you to do
> with us, Jesus of Nazareth? Have you come to destroy us? I
> know who you are, the Holy One of God." But Jesus rebuked
> him, saying, "Be silent, and come out of him!" And the unclean
> spirit, convulsing him and crying with a loud voice, came out
> of him. They were all amazed, and they kept on asking one
> another, "What is this? A new teaching—with authority! He
> commands even the unclean spirits, and they obey him. At
> once his fame began to spread throughout the surrounding
> region of Galilee. (Mark 1:21–28)

It has been said that change occurs when more authority is taken
than is given. And that is just what happens in this Gospel story.
Here is Jesus in the synagogue, where he is accepted as neither
teacher nor healer. He is one of us, a person in the pew. Jesus is
not even close to being on the radar as one who had the potential to be trained, commissioned or ordained to engage in such
spiritually powerful acts. So when Jesus calls the unclean spirit
out of the possessed person, people are astonished. How could
someone like Jesus—someone untrained, uneducated and unac-
cepted—act in the name of God?

Jesus definitely took more authority than was given him. We
see it all over the Gospels! He challenged the laws, the social con-
ventions and religious traditions of the day. By refusing to go
along with the status quo, by refusing to obey the law when it
demeaned or discounted a person, by refusing to reinforce
uneven and unjust power structures that attempted to maintain
inequality and entrench deep distinctions between gender, race
and caste, Jesus said, "No!"

In fact, in the very next passage of Mark's Gospel (1:29–31),
Jesus again refuses to go along with convention. In that passage,
Jesus is at Simon Peter's house. Simon's mother-in-law is ill with
a fever. In line with proper social convention for the period, the
men of the house intercede on her behalf. The text says, "...they
told him about her at once." Social and cultural custom dictated
that women remain in a separate part of the house while men
from outside the family were visiting.

At this point, conventional behavior ceases and Jesus, a male
outsider, goes to the sick woman, touches her and holds her

hand, and the fever leaves her. Jesus refused to comply with those
rules that separated him from others in any way. The Scriptures
contain a myriad of examples reiterating this point: Jesus refused
to abide by the law that forbade women from engaging in behaviors or roles reserved for men alone when he affirmed Mary's
place at his feet in the story of Martha and Mary. He refused to
conform again when he healed on the Sabbath. Again, taking
more authority than was given him, Jesus acted as gatekeeper and
stormed the temple area, driving out the vendors who were sell-
ing their goods there.

Over and over Jesus stands firm in what he knows to be the
truth—that we should be as one, one with God, one with each
other, one with all of creation. Jesus' relationship with God and
his ability to perceive the unity of all things is the foundation of
the authority he employs. Jesus' awareness of this communion
and refusal to perceive himself and others—especially the diseased and disenfranchised—as separate, supplied power to his
authority. After all, authority is not authority without power.

The concept of power is based on one's ability to stop the
mechanical process of conditioning and exert one's will in order
to change things. Real power overturns reality and forces a new
perspective. Think for a moment about how the life of the man
cited in the Gospel passage at the beginning of this section was
changed because of Jesus' action. Or call to mind the story of
Jesus stepping into the crowd gathered to stone the woman
caught in adultery. By taking more authority than he had been
given, Jesus asserts his power simply by commanding those gathered to let the one without sin cast the first stone. At that, the

woman's life was turned upside down; instead of meeting death, she experienced resurrection.

In her work, *Called to Question*, Joan Chittister suggests there is another side to power that Jesus knew, and that every woman, every child and every disenfranchised individual or community knows. It is the issue of powerlessness. Unfortunately, too often power becomes destructive when people, institutions and nations become too big, too strong, too overwhelming and too well-defended to be opposed, too politically well-positioned to be restrained or kept in check. This is the power that turns people into pawns and harnesses strength to serve slavery. To this misuse of power and authority, Jesus said, "No!"[2]

Certainly all of us have felt powerless to affect change and address the world's problems. In an era of famine and genocide, increasing violence and the build-up of nuclear weapons, feeling that we are at the mercy of politicians, presidents and global corporations, the question consciousness begs us to wrestle with is, "What can I possibly do about it?"

Believing that we have little or no power to affect change allows those who exercise power over us to keep it—unchecked and unchanged. Still it is difficult not to feel defeated when we have no way to find wiggle room, no connections to negotiate a deal, no inside track by which to put forth new ideas, work our will or bring forth a new vision.

For those of us concerned with spiritual growth and the pursuit of truth, the problem carries with it the very essence of integrity. How can I say I desire to follow the path of Jesus and do nothing about these things? How can we proclaim to belong to

Jesus Christ when we accept the status quo, conform without question or comply with traditions and codes of conduct that reinforce division, engage in oppression and thrive on inequality? If we desire to make Jesus' path our own, we cannot accept on any level that we are powerless. Jesus' life challenges us to the core to do something about these things. Like Jesus, we have to cultivate enough spiritual strength that we are able to refuse to go along with injustice. Refusing to go along with injustice is not easy. It means we can never pledge blind allegiance to anything, any person or any institution. If we want to follow the path of Jesus, we have to give ourselves to God and the pursuit of truth alone. We have to commit to engage the mind of Christ and bring forth the Christ consciousness in our own lives. The emergence of the Christ consciousness in our lives and in the world must become for Christians both the priority and benchmark of our lives. If the Christ consciousness is to come through us, it will take more than strength. It will also take power.

We plug into that power by grounding ourselves in the Word within and becoming familiar with what it feels like in heart, mind and body to be one with God and in communion with the great mystery. By cultivating knowledge of what this feels like and drawing our awareness to this union through a consistent practice of prayer, contemplation and engaging in acts of loving-kindness, we increase and strengthen our spiritual muscle.

Jesus did not pursue power for his own glorification, recognition or status. Jesus aligned the intention for his life with God's intention for his life—and it is in this alignment, in this connection that Jesus reveals the source and sustenance of real power and authority.

When we are able to cultivate and to rely on the power that comes from our union with God, we appropriate that power within us. We take it for our own and use it to do God's work here on earth. This is what Jesus did. And this is what we are called to do. Over and over Jesus tried to get the disciples to see that they, too, had the power and authority to do what he did. Jesus himself told the disciples, "[You] will also do the works that I do and...greater works than these" (John 14:12).

Transformation is the acme of the spiritual life, but lasting transformation can only come by being committed to the pursuit of freedom from ego, no matter what it costs. That kind of boundless courage can only come when we feel securely seated, held and hemmed in by God. The power and authority Jesus called upon for healing and offering forgiveness was drawn from his relationship with God. Our relationship with God promises the same for us.

Being firmly rooted in his relationship with God propelled Jesus' ministry and gave him courage to challenge the status quo and refuse injustice. This is the same power and authority to which Jesus calls us. But if we are to be strong enough to refuse injustice, we, like Jesus, have to develop a deeply intimate relationship with God. Only then will we possess the strength and courage to refuse evil and the power and authority to transform it.

Drawing on his relationship with God, Jesus refused to endure evil and engaged in God's work of healing and justice. Jesus used his gifts with power and authority everywhere he went and whenever they were needed. He used the gifts given him by God in the synagogue, in the homes of women, on the streets, at the

Samaritan's well, in the company of tax collectors and prostitutes. Jesus did not wait for someone to grant him permission to use his gifts when and where he did. He gave himself to God's work regardless of what others thought of him, regardless of the consequences such actions brought forth or the difficulties that stood in his way.

Until we develop the kind of intimate relationship with God that gives rise to the power and authority necessary in order to refuse evil and engage in God's work of justice and healing, the Christ consciousness does not stand a chance of breaking through our hearts, penetrating humanity's consciousness or pervading the planet.

PRACTICE

Ego Identification Exercise

At the end of your day, take a few minutes to bring your mind and body to stillness. Replay the events of your day. Note the times and circumstances in which you overreacted or underreacted. What would have been different had you followed Moses' example at the burning bush and stopped, looked and listened prior to reacting?

In your journal write about a time when you were able to successfully employ the three rules of observation: stop, look and listen. How do you suppose the situation would have unfolded had you not been able to employ these commands? What did you learn that you may have missed if you weren't willing to observe the situation without judgment?

Contemplation

Jesus asked the two blind men who approached him for healing, "Do you believe that I can do this?" The blind men responded, "Yes, Lord." Then Jesus touched their eyes and said, "Let it be done to you according to your faith."

Use your journal to explore what beliefs you hold about your own healing or your own capacity for change. Consider those areas of your life that need healing or changing. Write down your own response to Jesus' question, "Do you believe that I can do this?"

Prayer

Divine One, bringer of healing energy and light, let your power flow through me and energize me throughout my day. Keep me close to the source of your radiant being and open me to Wisdom's presence and surprises. Amen.

Action of Loving-kindness

Send a note or an e-mail to someone from your past who believed in you. Tell them what kind of difference their belief in you made in your ability to succeed or get through that time in your life.

CHAPTER SEVEN

Two by Two

Then he went about among the villages teaching. He called the twelve and began to send them out two by two, and gave them authority over the unclean spirits. (Mark 6:6b–7)

The Christ consciousness emerges within and through our relationships. Relationships provide an arena that allows us to explore the depths of self, others and God. Loving relationships, at their best, provide a home and refuge to which we can return time and again when transformation has taken its toll and we are weary from traveling the spiritual journey. Having a companion or friend with whom we can share the journey of life can ease the burden of becoming.

We need other people on this journey. It is not a journey we make alone. We need others to give us a word of encouragement when times get tough. We need others to pick us up when life delivers a heavy blow. We need others to comfort us, hold us and push us forward when necessary. It is human nature to desire another to enter our experience. We all need partners in this life.

We who claim Jesus' path as our own are on a mission together. Our mission is to love. To love fiercely. To love not just those who are easy for us to love, but to learn to love even our enemies. This mission can only be accomplished in and through our relationships. There is no love without involvement. Love is always a two-dimensional process and because of that nothing in the universe is irrelevant to us. We are in relationship with absolutely all of it. Our relationship with God is expressed in the way we relate to one another, care for one another, the earth that provides for us and the cosmos that envelope us.

To love fiercely and allow ourselves to be loved fiercely, this is our life's mission and the means to our transformation. We can only bring forth the Christ consciousness by giving and receiving love. Giving and receiving love is the breath of the soul. It is what makes the soul open up and learn to fly.

Jesus sent the disciples out two by two because he knew that every single one of our relationships is dependent upon our relationship with God. The fullness of life is not a private affair. It is not an individual experience. We need other people to crash into and rub up against so we can learn to love in many dimensions and at all levels of our life. To love and be loved—that's why Jesus sent them out in twos.

Having a friend, companion or partner allowed the disciples to rely on each other. When one was down, the other could lead. When one was in doubt, the other was there to remind the one in doubt of God's mysterious ways. Jesus sent them out in twos so they could say to each other, "Remember when..." and be reminded, even in the most difficult circumstances, that we do get through suffering and all things come to pass. Having someone with whom we share the journey can make even the most oppressive situations bearable. Joan Chittister articulates well the profound impact of having another with whom we can share the journey. She writes,

> Knowing that someone else knows where you are, feels the way you feel, does—for me at least—really "take back yesterday." It smoothes whatever scars were suffered there. It is being alone in my pain, my fear, the burden of my memories, that presses my face to the ground. But when one person says, "I know,"... "I understand,"..."I can see why you feel that way," I become whole again. Sane. Mature. It is the humanity of the other that brings my humanity back to life.[1]

Jesus sent them out in twos because he understood that all of life and all living is relational. Jesus himself showed us that the kingdom is not a place. It is an experience. It is the experience of acceptance when you were just sure you would be rejected. It is the surprise of getting something right on intuition. It is the feeling of being heard—just heard. Not reacted to, but heard. Not advised, just heard. It is the feeling of being received in love when you were just sure you had ruined everything this time. It is the ability to share laughter when you were just sure you had made a fool of yourself. It is the feeling of another's arms holding you tight just when you thought you would be turned away.

Every aspect of our lives—our religious practice, our spiritual and emotional growth, even our basic survival—is impossible without other people. We are partners in this mission of transformation. We are here to help one another respond wholeheartedly to love, wholeheartedly to life's challenges and God's call to become more than we are. We are here to help one another respond from love and with love at all times and to all people.

Treasuring One Another

> Jesus...got up from the table, took off his outer robe, and tied a towel around himself. Then he poured water into a basin and began to wash the disciple's feet and to wipe them with the towel that was tied around him.... I have set you an example, that you also should do as I have done to you. (John 13:4–5, 15)

"You should do as I have done to you." Over and over again, Jesus said through his words and actions, "Do what I do." This was not solely a command for the disciples, it is also a command directed to us. The point of transformation is to bring forth from within the highest expression of the Christ consciousness possible which is communion—being one with each other, all of creation and God. We are called to become the eyes and ears, heart and flesh of God right here, right now, just as Jesus was when he walked the earth.

By joining eye to eye, heart to heart, flesh to flesh we engage in the path of transformation together. Jesus' presence, the Christ consciousness, is manifest through our relationships and the way we treat one another. Not just in how we accept one another, but also in how we let go of one another. Perhaps Jesus washes his friend's feet on the eve of his crucifixion as a way of letting go and saying good-bye. He shows us that even in this—even in parting—we can love one another and treasure one another and the gifts our lives have brought one another.

Washing the disciples' feet reveals how deeply Jesus truly treasured them. "Being treasured" has something to do with intimacy, with being next to or really "with" someone, joined in heart, mind and spirit. Still, intimacy is not a perpetual state of being. It is a transitory experience. There are intimate moments, not eras of intimacy. And intimacy is not necessarily only the result of a long relationship. Rather, it can be the momentary insight or recognition that you and I are one, deeply connected with God, and interconnected with all of creation.

Still there are times when all of us feel alone, untethered and disconnected in our relationships. We can be in a crowd of people. We can be gathered with family and friends. We can be at home, work or church and still feel completely alone, isolated and disconnected—even from those we love.

Jesus spent his life trying to bridge the gaps between people by sidling up to those people most likely to feel alone, isolated and left out. He let people know with a touch or a word or a breath that he was with them. He had a way of reminding people that they were not alone. He conveyed to those who felt less-than that they were enough.

We only have to recall Jesus' actions with the woman caught in adultery to get a clear indication of what is required of us. Remember, Jesus said to those who were armed with stones, "Let the one without sin cast the first stone." At that, the crowd dispersed and the woman's life was saved. Jesus did not allow the life of this woman, which others had deemed worthless, sinful and corrupt, to be snuffed out. By inserting himself in the situation and standing with the condemned woman, Jesus' actions freed her from death's grip and quite literally gave her a new lease on life.

Anytime we experience this kind of love and acceptance, this kind of willingness by others to put themselves on the line for us, this kind connectedness and intimacy, we experience the Christ consciousness. This is what the Christ consciousness is—the awareness that you are me and I am you and we are one. It's the feeling that we are not alone, breaking through the thick illusion that we are separate. It is a deep trust that your life and my life matter—not just for oneself, one's family or one's own accomplishment, but for the conscious evolution and development of humanity as a whole.

Throughout his life, Jesus stood with those who were unwelcome, unwanted, displaced or disenfranchised. He was a companion to those who were otherwise unaccompanied. Jesus spent his life standing next to those who felt ostracized and found themselves on the fringes of society. He did not offer his company, healing, food or drink with grandiose gestures or attention-seeking gimmicks. He simply sat next to others, shared a moment of intimacy and connection with them and let them know they were welcome to be his companions.

For us, as for Jesus, the Christ consciousness reveals itself when we move toward one another—regardless of disagreements, offenses or disappointments—to say, "Hey, I'm with you in this. Don't forget I love you." The Christ consciousness comes through us when we affirm others or are affirmed ourselves—in times of doubt or despair—that we are enough just as we are.

Jesus began what became his Last Supper with the washing of his disciple's feet. He showed them and us, one last time, that we are meant to do as he did and bring forth the Christ consciousness through our relationships and the way we treat one another. Eye to eye. Heart to heart. Flesh to flesh. This is the only way the kingdom will come.

MAKING LOVE

Six days before the Passover Jesus came to Bethany, the home of Lazarus, whom he had raised from the dead. There they gave a dinner for him. Martha served, and Lazarus was one of those at the table with him. Mary took a pound of costly perfume made of pure nard, anointed Jesus' feet, and wiped them with her hair. The house was filled with the fragrance of the perfume. But Judas Iscariot, one of his disciples (the one who was about to betray him), said, "Why was this perfume not sold for three hundred denarii and the money given to the poor?" (He said this not because he cared about the poor, but because he was a thief; he kept the common purse and used to steal what was put into it.) Jesus said, "Leave her alone. She bought it so that she might keep it for the day of my burial. You always have the poor with you, but you do not always have me." (John 12:1–7)

In John's Gospel, just prior to Jesus entering Jerusalem, we find the story of Mary interrupting a dinner Jesus is having with Lazarus and some others. In this account, Mary's anointing of Jesus takes place just prior to his entering Jerusalem to crowds waving palms. The Scripture tells us that Mary anoints Jesus the day before he climbs onto that colt and meets his destiny.

It seems that Mary and Jesus shared something rather intimate and unspoken that the others just did not get. Remember, she had been supporting Jesus' ministry for some time. She too had followed him, listened to him and watched him. She knows from her own experience with Jesus that he is no ordinary man. He initiates conversations and seeks out the company of women in an age when that was frowned on or forbidden. She was with Jesus when he wept at Lazarus's tomb and then raised him from the dead. She knew Jesus had tax collectors, zealots and other shady characters for friends. He brought them to her house for dinner! And she knew that the scribes and Pharisees tried to use these relationships as fuel for discrediting Jesus and accusing him of political posturing against Roman rule.

Still Jesus continued. He continued his relationships with women, children, tax collectors and sinners. And not only that, but his shady friends probably gave him a hard time because he associated with "conservatives" or "traditionalists" like Jarius, one of the synagogue officials, whose daughter he healed, and Nicodemus, a member of the Sanhedrin, who came to see Jesus under the cover of night so as not to be seen in public with him.

Mary may have well been a witness to his courage and his commitment to integrity—to living by his conscience rather than blindly accepting tradition, or even the opinions of his friends. When Mary anointed Jesus' feet, it was a profound expression of intimacy and understanding. It was an act of lovemaking.

Rumi said, "The way you make love is the way God will be with you."[2] And yet too often we react like Peter to Jesus' attempts to wash his feet—resisting another's generous act of love or, going to the other extreme, as Peter does when he finally concedes and says, "OK, Jesus, go ahead and get my feet, and while you're at it, get my hands and head too."

Jesus insists that is not the way to love either. Expecting God to do it all, expecting God to do all the work of our transformation is not loving. It is receiving. Expecting God to do what we can do for ourselves is not how we trod the path of transformation. It is not even the stuff of faith. It is selfish. It is indulgent. It denies the relational aspect of our relationship with God.

The interaction between Jesus and Mary in this passage reveals that love is about being engaged. Engaged in the relationship. Engaged in the giving and receiving. Engaged in the one act of sharing. If one is always receiving, or if one is always giving, it's not love. It's playing it safe. Love is about taking risks and allowing ourselves to be vulnerable with another. Think about Jesus washing Peter's feet while knowing that Peter will betray him later. Or think about Jesus receiving Judas's kiss, knowing this act will hand him over to the Roman authorities.

Jesus continued to love them even though they would not be there for him later. Jesus did not withhold—even from those who, in the end, would turn on him or act as if they never knew him. He continued to share who he was and all he had even knowing it would not change his fate, knowing that those he loved, those he gave himself to, would not be able to go the distance with him.

Love is about exploring the depths of passion and compassion until something new emerges between us. It is about opening even when we are vulnerable and even when it hurts. It is about sharing what we have even if that means there will be nothing left over.

Love, even in our relationship with God, requires us to be more than passive recipients. We have to be engaged in the giving *and* receiving. We are partners with God in this lovemaking. By its very nature it is an act of sharing. It is an expression of selflessness and intimacy. And the way we bring ourselves to this union, the way we give ourselves to others and the way we receive others is indicative of the way we are with God. Sharing lavishly, unexpectedly, when it's a sacrifice to do so, when it goes against our nature to do so—this is what lovemaking is about. This is how we and the world we live in will be transformed by love. The more difficult the act of sharing in which we participate, the greater the opportunity for the Christ consciousness to be unleashed. Don't forget—"The way you make love is the way God will be with you."

Practice

Ego Identification Exercise

Emotions born of ego constantly control and imprison us. They slow us down and prevent us from engaging in transformation. This imprisonment takes many forms: We're imprisoned by our desire for material things. We're held in bondage by our reactive whims and egocentric desires. We're held captive by our careers, relationships, fears and doubts. We're prisoners to other people's perception of us. We're incarcerated by our own desperate need for other people's acceptance.

Today, pay attention to the emotions that motivate you and influence your interactions with others. Begin to identify when you have responded to a person or situation from the standpoint of ego and when you were able to respond from the confidence of the Word within. In the evening, review your daily activities and interactions. Was the Christ consciousness able to come through you? If so, how? If not, why?

Contemplation

After washing the disciples' feet, Jesus said, "I have set you an example, that you also should do as I have done to you." Consider how you emulated Jesus' example today. How did you show others that you treasured them?

Prayer

God of power and strength, changer of what seems changeless, help me to find my strength, power and authority in you. Grant me the desire and will to change the conditioned patterns of my existence. Reveal to me how my strength can unite with yours, that I may become all that you created me to be. Amen.

Action of Loving-kindness

This week show someone that you really treasure them. Surprise your spouse, a friend or neighbor and cook his or her favorite meal. Volunteer to clean the kitchen afterward, too.

CHAPTER EIGHT

WE GO TOGETHER INTO EVERYTHING

Immediately he made the disciples get into the boat and go on ahead to the other side, while he dismissed the crowds. And after he had dismissed the crowds, he went up the mountain by himself to pray. When evening came, he was there alone, but by this time the boat, battered by the waves, was far from the land, for the wind was against them. And early in the morning he came walking toward them on the sea. But when the disciples saw him walking on the sea, they were terrified, saying, "It is a ghost!" And they cried out in fear. But immediately Jesus spoke to them and said, "Take heart, it is I; do not be afraid."

Peter answered him, "Lord, if it is you, command me to come to you on the water." He said, "Come." So Peter got out of the boat, started walking on the water, and came toward Jesus. But when he noticed the strong wind, he became frightened, and beginning to sink, he cried out, "Lord, save me!" Jesus immediately reached out his hand and caught him, saying to him, "You of little faith, why did you doubt?" When they got into the boat, the wind ceased. (Matthew 14:22–32)

None among us escapes this life without incurring numerous metaphorical storms, earthquakes and strong winds that threaten to uproot and destroy the sense we have of ourselves, the nature of life and even our belief in God. An experience of loss, grief, insecurity or difficulty in our relationships can be the source of such storms. But all too often our confidence in the fact that we are hemmed into God is shaken by something much smaller than the big storms of life. We easily lose our footing when a derogatory comment is made about us, rumors threaten our reputation, we get in an argument with someone we love or we are rejected by someone from whom we want approval and acceptance.

These smaller disturbances, if we allow them, can erode our confidence and chip away at our belief that we are hemmed into God. They can distract us and make it more difficult for us to encounter ourselves as one with God. As a result, we often forget that at our essence we are so united with God that God is closer to us than our own breath. At our essence we are indestructible, invincible and untouchable by all but God alone because the ground of all being is the Word of God.

To be sure, the storms and strong winds of life can yank us off course or become roadblocks on the path of transformation. A fight with a friend, a disagreement in opinion with our spouse or a personal failure such as an inappropriate display of emotions, or even an argument over something inconsequential can cause enough noise or disturbance in our lives that it drowns out the whispers of God and distracts us from pursuing the path to which God has called us.

Remember, in the Gospel story of Jesus feeding the five thousand, when the disciples approached Jesus concerned that those gathered should be sent away so they could procure food, Jesus commanded the disciples: "You give them something to eat" (Matthew 14:16). But the disciples did not believe that they had the ability to do what Jesus did. They did not believe they had within their means the power and authority to change the circumstances or address the hunger of the people. The disciples continued to look to Jesus, to look outside of themselves for the power necessary to withstand the storms of life. And this is where the disciples, and we too, miss the point of pursuing the path of Jesus.

Can we withstand the storms of life and stand firm on the promise of Jesus to be with us always? Or are we like Peter in this passage, focused on what seems impossible even though Jesus is in his sight? Can we hang in there when the pressure is on and still remain grounded in God's word? Do we begin to sink the minute we struggle? Do we crumble when presented with difficult circumstances or people? The struggles of life challenge us to develop enough inner strength and spiritual muscle that we can stand in the storms of life and not be moved from knowing that God is with us, that God will reach out and catch us.

When we give into doubt and fear, the ego wins and the Word within is silenced or drowned out by the ego's insistence that we do not have what it takes to negotiate the waters of life! The path of transformation challenges us to surface belief in ourselves and trust in the presence of God at all times. Life challenges us to develop stamina so we can withstand the pressure of the passing storms, stand on the firing line and not shrink back. But in order to do that we have to tether ourselves to something. We have to cling to something. Root ourselves in something.

That something is the Word of God alive in our hearts. It is the small still voice, the tiny whispering sound Elijah heard when he stood at the cave entrance on Mount Horeb (1 Kings 19:12). It is the presence of Jesus in you and in me. It's the voice or sense that wells up in us when we become conscious that God is with us always.

We have to do whatever it takes to plug into the voice of Jesus that says, "Very truly, I tell you, the one who believes in me will also do the works that I do and, in fact, will do greater works than these..." (John 14:12). Jesus never asked for worship. He invited people to follow him. To do what he did. To live wholly conscious of our union with God. To go into every aspect of life committed to truth, committed to love, committed to revealing the power that comes when we tether ourselves to God alone.

This is why Jesus questions Peter, "Why do you doubt? Why do you doubt that you can do what I do? Why do you doubt that you too are made in the image and likeness of God? Why do you doubt your ability to be who you are made to be? Why do you doubt your ability to feed the world's deep hungers?"

All too often we give ourselves more readily to the storms of life, to the voices (internal or external) that say, "You are less-than..." instead of giving ourselves to the thoughts that reinforce the voice of God that says, "I am with you. Don't be afraid. We go together into all things."

It is so easy to get caught up in the storms of life. It is so easy to lose our footing when being confronted with negativity, unfairly criticized or bombarded by the bombshells that befall us as we trod the transformative path. The challenge is for each of us to develop a certain trust that we cannot be separated from God no matter the reality we confront, the mistakes we make or the tyrants we face.

Prayer, contemplation and acts of loving-kindness keep us rooted in the presence of God, providing solid ground on which we can stand even in the face of life's difficulties. Like Elijah at the entrance to the cave, these practices bring us to the place of sheer silence, absolute stillness of thought, feeling and emotion. There we find the opening to the unknown, the gateway to God, the passageway to freedom.

IF NOT NOW, THEN WHEN?

On the third day there was a wedding in Cana of Galilee, and the mother of Jesus was there. Jesus and his disciples had also been invited to the wedding. When the wine gave out, the mother of Jesus said to him, "They have no wine." And Jesus said to her, "Woman, what concern is that to you and to me? My hour has not yet come." His mother said to the servants, "Do whatever he tells you." Now standing there were six stone water jars for the Jewish rites of purification, each holding twenty or thirty gallons. Jesus said to them, "Fill the jars with water." And they filled them up to the brim. He said to them, "Now draw some out, and take it to the chief steward." So they took it. When the steward tasted the water that had become wine, and did not know where it came from (though the servants who had drawn the water knew), the steward called the bridegroom and said to him, "Everyone serves the good wine

first, and then the inferior wine after the guests have become
drunk. But you have kept the good wine until now." Jesus did
this, the first of his signs, in Cana of Galilee, and revealed his
glory; and his disciples believed in him. (John 2:1–11)

Transformation is not something we can put off. Sometimes we
are confronted with a situation on our transformative journey
that demands something of us we have yet to discover in ourselves or some gift or ability we have yet to share with others. We
grow and develop as the demands of life require it of us.

In the story of the wedding at Cana, Mary doesn't wait around
for Jesus to *feel* ready. Like a good mom, Mary gives Jesus the push
he needs to step into his vocation. When a situation arises in
which her son's particular gifts are needed, Mary does not allow
Jesus to avoid the predicament she knows he can remedy. In a
way, she is saying to Jesus, "Don't miss this opportunity to use
your gifts. You need to do this!"

This is not one of Jesus' best moments. When Mary comes to
him and says there is no more wine, his reply is stealthy. He says,
"Woman, what concern is that to you and to me? My hour has
not yet come." Jesus, it seems, has an attitude. He is basically saying, "So? I'm not ready to do what you want me to do." But Mary
disregards his hesitancy and, in effect, says, "The time is now!"
when she says to the servers, "Do whatever he tells you."

What a message for us! Sometimes we can't wait for the
moment to "feel" right. We can't wait until everything unfolds
and there are no other options. We have to be willing, and sometimes forced by the circumstances of life, to step up to the plate
like Jesus did—even before we might feel ready to do so.

As his mother, Mary probably knew that Jesus had to take this initial step of changing water into wine before he could begin to explore his deeper capacities—for transformation and healing and calling forth life from the most deserted places. Just as she did when she said "yes" to God.

Mary's "yes" was just the beginning, just as it is for us. After saying yes, she still had to give birth. She had to manifest what God conceived in her. And Mary knew that Jesus needed to manifest the dream God had conceived in him. She knew that he had to bring his divine nature from within—just as she did in giving birth to him. Mary pushes Jesus to do what he knows, deep down, he can do—he has to do.

From this moment on, Jesus moves into his life trying to teach the disciples and others how to do the same thing. He encourages them to reach beyond their current capabilities and explore deeper capacities for healing and letting go and bringing forth new life.

Jesus' life challenges us to explore our own deeper capacities for change and transformation in ourselves, our relationships and the institutions in which we work. We are also challenged to call forth in others their deeper potential. Again, John's Gospel tells us that Jesus said, "...the one who believes in me will also do the works I do and, in fact, will do greater works than these" (14:12).

Jesus reinforces this conviction when he says later in the same passage, "You [are] in me and I [am] in you" (14:20). With this, Jesus is urging us to believe that we can do what he did. To become what he became! This is how we remember Jesus. This is how the broken body of Christ will be made whole. This is how

healing and transformation will come about—when we commit
to becoming what we know we are deep down, an equal member
in the Body of Christ.

As pilgrims on the journey to becoming, we have to change
and grow and move out of our comfort zones in order to access
our deeper potential. The spiritual life challenges us to move
beyond what we think we are capable of—in order for our
deeper capacities to emerge and evolve into their fullest expression. This journey constantly calls us to embrace a larger context
for our lives.

The apostle Paul makes the same challenge when he claims we
are many parts, but all one body. In his First Letter to the
Corinthians, Paul writes, "For just as the body is one and has
many members, and all the members of the body, though many,
are one body, so it is with Christ" (12:12). Claiming the gifts God
planted in us and calling forth the gifts of all who desire a greater
expression of wholeness and unity in our world is how we begin
to heal the brokenness in ourselves and our world. When every
one of us claims our power to transform and be transformed, to
heal and be healed, to feed and be fed, we become bread for the
world and the Christ consciousness emerges through us!

Jesus' whole life was a journey of transformation—from being
driven to the wilderness, to his first miracle at the wedding feast
of Cana, through his travels from town to town, healing people
and challenging them to higher potential and deeper levels of car-
ing. From telling the crippled man who could not stand on his
own two feet to take up his mat and go home, to calling Lazarus
out of the tomb and insisting that those gathered as community

unbind him and set him free. All the way to the cross, where he continued to entrust himself to God's hands, and on into the resurrection when he said to Mary in the garden, "Do not cling to me." Transformation, by its very nature, does not allow us to remain staid in our relationship to life, in our relationship with God or our relationships with one another.

So we must ask ourselves, "How are we being called to transformation? How does this point in time, and the circumstances we find ourselves in, challenge us to explore our deeper capacities for doing what Jesus did? In what ways are we being called to become a fuller expression of love, healing and forgiveness? What are our deeper capacities for transforming our lives, our church and our world?"

The path of Jesus challenges us to grow beyond what we think is our fullest capacity to discover the unexplored and untapped potential so needed if we are ever going to address the critical and yet unmet needs of others, the famines that touch those not only starved for physical nourishment, but even those who are starved for acceptance, inclusion and companionship. Our world needs the benefit of our transformation now! If not now, then when? If not today, then when?

FIGHT ON!

On the third new moon after the Israelites had gone out of the land of Egypt, on that very day, they came into the wilderness of Sinai. They had journeyed from Rephidim, entered the wilderness of Sinai, and camped in the wilderness; Israel camped there in front of the mountain. Then Moses went up to God; the LORD called to him from the mountain, saying, "Thus you shall say to the house of Jacob, and tell the Israelites: You have seen what I did to the Egyptians, and how I bore you on eagles' wings and brought you to myself. Now therefore, if you obey my voice and keep my covenant, you shall be my treasured possession out of all the peoples. Indeed, the whole earth is mine, but you shall be for me a priestly kingdom and a holy nation. These are the words that you shall speak to the Israelites." (Exodus 19:1–6)

In this story we hear that the children of Israel arrive at Sinai and its surrounding area, called the "wilderness of Sinai." Everything that transpires from the beginning of chapter 19 through the rest of Exodus, all of Leviticus and Numbers up through 10:10 is connected with this area.

With deliverance accomplished, the people now find themselves encamped before the holy mountain. While the Exodus of Egypt marked the birth of Israel as a geographical nation, the experience at Sinai provides the birth of Israel as a spiritual people.

It's here at Sinai that God is revealed to the people. It's here that God enters into the covenant with them. It's here at Sinai that God lays out the terms of the agreement—the laws that are to govern Israel's existence. We learn from their experience at Sinai that revelation, covenant and law are the bedrock upon which the community of Israel is built.

Revelation, the self-disclosure of God, is neither new in the Bible story as told up until now nor unknown in the archives of other religions. The revelation that takes place at Sinai, however, is distinct in that it takes place before a community of people, who then act upon what they have seen and heard.

The events in Exodus 19 contain some of the best-known images in the Torah. God's protection of Israel is likened to their being carried "on eagle's wings." The people are distinguished as God's "treasured possession," and they are challenged to go all out, to give everything they have to the task of becoming a "kingdom of priests and a holy nation." Another characteristic that distinguishes the giving of this Law from those in other accounts is the unity of the revelation. The one breath from which all life emanates, the eternal "I AM" to which all belong, speaks.

This is the same one who says, "Hear, O Israel, the Lord is One!" There is no dualism. This Law rejects the worship of many gods. It contradicts the religions and philosophies of other ancient cultures that saw a god in every heavenly body, tree and rock, and asserts that there is but one God. All the world's goodness—the power of the sun, the beauty of the trees and the permanence of the rock—comes from its creator, the one God.

It took great courage for the people of Israel to maintain this belief during their forty years of wandering in the wilderness, during the long ages when they were conquered by other nations with their many gods. But they knew the truth of what they had found and fought to keep it, fought to hand it down generation after generation, making it the most important element of what it meant to be the people of God.

If the journey of becoming is the least bit important to us, we've got to fight on. If we believe that we too are called to be a priestly people dedicated to pursuing the utter and total transformation of heart and soul that Jesus was about, we've got to fight on. If we believe that we are all children of God and all of us are God's treasured possessions whether we are male or female, Jew or Greek, slave or free, gay or straight, black or white, Appalachian or Hispanic, Muslim, Jew or Christian, we've got to fight on.

If we believe that the things that separate us are superficial and that we are called to live from a greater perspective and larger context in which we never forget that there is only one life from which all life comes, one breath that animates all life, we've got to fight on. If we believe that coming to the eucharistic table, where no one is turned away is the highest expression of the Christ consciousness on earth and something that we aspire to in all areas of our lives, we've got to fight on.

We've got to envision a new life together. We've got to have the courage to sow new seeds that will produce a new harvest from which we can feed and be fed. God has a plan for each one of us. This we can trust. We must not grow complacent. We have to retire such attitudes revealed in statements like, "It will never work." "We've tried this in the past and nothing ever changes." "I don't know if I have it in me to start over, to try again to address the issues that separate us."

I say to you, "What else is there?" If we are forever saying, "I can't start over," or "Nothing will ever change," if we are forever trying to hold onto what we have and what we know, change will never happen. Jesus' life, death and resurrection demand that we consider the possibility that change and transformation is not only where we meet God, but it is also the vehicle through which we become what God intends us to be.

Remember, the Israelites were camping at Sinai! This was a temporary place for them. The Promised Land could only be reached if they were willing to move away from this holy mountain, this place where God was revealed to them. And that is difficult. But we have to do the same thing.

If we are ever going to get to the Promised Land, we've got to be willing to move. If we are ever going to experience resurrection, we have got to let go of the life we know. We've got to embrace a vision worth dying for. That's the call for us now: to discover that vision, to find our heart's desire as individuals, as a community and as humanity as a whole and pursue it with everything we've got.

If great possibility lays at the heart of God, at the heart of the universe, the heart even of the spiritual journey itself, then we've got to enter the same sea of possibility that Moses entered when he led the Israelites out of slavery. We've got to enter the same sea of possibility that Jesus entered when he showed us the way to freedom, reconciliation and resurrection. We've got to enter the sea of possibility that inspires visionaries, prophets and trailblazers. We've got to enter the sea of possibility that calls us into new ways of being God's people, new ways of working for justice, new ways of bringing light into the world, new ways of setting captives free, new ways of feeding the hungry, curing the ill, driving out demons, new ways of bringing forth the kingdom!

PRACTICE

Ego Identification Exercise

All the negative traits that we so easily see in others are merely a reflection of our own negative traits. Bring to mind a person who gets under your skin, irritates you or someone you go out of your way to avoid. Take some time to journal about the traits in this person that bother you. Then, for each trait you've identified, write down times when this same trait has shown itself in you. Identify ways you can transform these negative traits in yourself.

Contemplation

Consider the story of Mary and Jesus at the wedding feast in Cana. What gifts do you feel remain untapped in you? What circumstances are pushing you to explore new or deeper capacities in yourself? How are you embracing the opportunities to use your gifts?

Prayer

God of birth, death and resurrection, renew my eagerness to pursue the path of transformation. Do not let me procrastinate any longer. Help me to discover the unexplored and untapped potential that resides in me. Fulfill my desire to give my life completely to the greater good for the whole of humanity. Help me evolve! Amen.

Action of Loving-kindness

For one week, act on every single thought of generosity that arises spontaneously in your heart, and notice what happens as a consequence.

CHAPTER ONE

1. Eckhart Tolle, *A New Earth: Awakening to Your Life's Purpose* (New York: Dutton, 2005), pp. 12, 13.
2. Yehuda Berg, *The Power of Kabbalah* (Los Angeles: Kabbalah Centre International, 2004), p. 116.
3. Tolle, p. 13.
4. Tolle, p. 13.

CHAPTER TWO

1. Coleman Barks, trans. *The Essential Rumi* (San Francisco: Harper Collins, 1995), p. 247.
2. Joan Chittister, O.S.B., *Listen with the Heart* (New York: Sheed & Ward, 2003), p. 35.
3. Thomas Merton, *New Seeds of Contemplation* (New York: New Directions, 1972), pp. 25, 26.
4. Basil Pennington, *Centering Prayer: Renewing an Ancient Christian Prayer Form* (New York: Doubleday, 1980), p. 65.
5. Pennington, p. 70.

CHAPTER THREE

1. Matthew Fox, *Meditations with Meister Eckhart* (Santa Fe: Bear & Co., 1982), p. 28.
2. Barks, p. 141.
3. Merton, p. 3.
4. Clayborne Carson, ed., *The Autobiography of Martin Luther King, Jr.* (New York: Warner, 1998), p. 362.

CHAPTER FOUR

1. Andrew Cohen, *The Eternal Present,* July 3, 2004. Available at http://www.andrewcohen.org/quote.

CHAPTER FIVE

1. Matthew Fox, *Original Blessing* (Santa Fe: Bear and Co., 1983), p. 160.

CHAPTER SIX

1. Barks, p. 36.
2. See Joan Chittister, *Called to Question* (New York: Sheed & Ward, 2004), p. 141.

CHAPTER SEVEN

1. Chittister, *Listen With the Heart,* p. 103.
2. Barks, p.185.